THE BRAIN HEALTH

& BETTER MEMORY BOOK

IMPROVE FOCUS, MEMORY RECALL, AND PREVENT DEMENTIA

Howard VanEs, M.A.

The Brain Health & Better Memory Book
Improve Focus, Memory Recall, and Prevent Dementia

Howard VanEs, M.A.

Published by:
BooksOnHealth.net

ISBN: 978-0692392218

Disclaimer: The information and ideas presented in this book are for educational purposes only. This book is not intended to be a substitute for consulting with an appropriate health care provider. Any changes or additions to your medical care should be discussed with your physician. The author and publisher disclaim any liability arising directly or indirectly from this book.

TABLE OF CONTENTS

Introduction

Chapter 1 - The big picture:
what affects our brains 7

Chapter 2 - A look inside:
how our brains age 21

Chapter 3 - Food for thought:
how diet affects brain health 37

Chapter 4 - A little extra help:
supplements 53

Chapter 5 - Move it or lose it:
exercise and brain health 87

Chapter 6 - This is your brain;
this is your brain on stress 99

Chapter 7 - We are social animals:
the importance of social connections 125

Chapter 8 - ZZZZZs:
sleep is very good for your brain 139

Chapter 9 - Om:
yoga as an antidote to aging. 161

Additional publications of interest 169

About the author 175

Your brain plays a major role in almost everything you do.

INTRODUCTION

The human brain is an amazing and fascinating organ. It weighs in at approximately 3 percent of your body weight and receives one quarter of its blood flow. Interestingly, there are no two brains alike in the world. Your interpretation of the last hit on the radio differs from how other people experience it, and the same goes for anything you read, see, or experience.

Your brain plays a major role in almost everything you do including thinking, feeling, communicating, breathing, remembering, working, playing, sleeping, etc. Vital to the quality of life, therefore, is maintaining or improving the health of your brain.

The reduction or loss of brain function can result in any number of problems, including forgetfulness, moodiness, insomnia, lack of problem-solving skills, and an inability to communicate effectively. When brain health deterioration becomes more severe, it can lead to dementia and the problems associated with this serious decline, including confusion, difficulty understanding visual images, changes in personality, trouble remembering, hallucinations, and lack of judgment.

As we mature, there are any number of factors that can affect your overall brain health and memory, including health issues, medications, diet, activity/exercise, stress levels, sleep or lack of it, social connections, and how mentally active you are. This book will address these issues, explaining how each impacts the health of your brain, and then offer ideas, tips, and tools to optimize the health of your brain and your memory.

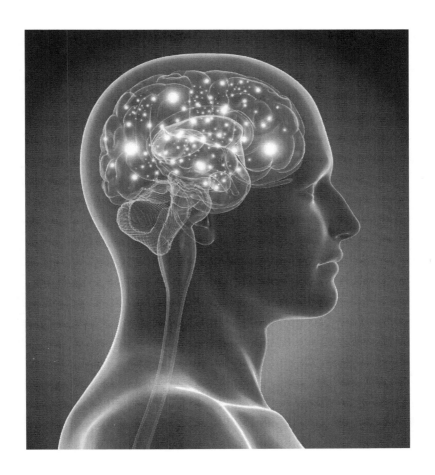

Chapter 1

THE BIG PICTURE

WHAT AFFECTS OUR BRAINS

*As you age, the toll of all the **nutrition choices** you made throughout your life is reflected in your brain's health.*

The health of our brains are influenced by a number of different factors and this chapter will give you a brief overview of them. Subsequent chapters will go into more detail.

Influence of diet on brain health

From the moment you are born, the growth of your brain is heavily dependent on your diet. Fats and proteins are the building blocks used by the brain to expand all its nerve cells, called dendrites. The nervous system is kind of like a network connecting various parts through electrical impulses. Myelin, a fatty substance, is the covering material for all of the nervous system, which facilitates proper signal transmission. Diseases such as multiple sclerosis (MS), are known as "demyelinating" diseases since their critical feature is the loss of the insulating material, the myelin, on the nerve fiber. Currently, studies are raising concerns about signs that more and more children are displaying a reduction in myelin, a result attributed to an emphasis on fat-free diets.

As you age, the toll of all the nutrition choices you made throughout your life is reflected in your brain's health. In chapter three, the role of nutrition is explored more fully including which foods detract from brain health and which nutrients should be included in your diet to optimize brain function.

Medications

Many commonly prescribed medications interfere with brain health and memory, and for chronic users, the damage of these drugs can be severe and very dangerous. The top three drug families that can affect your brain are:

1) Anti-anxiety drugs: Benzodiazepines, for example, reduce activity in parts of the brain and have a sedative effect as well as muscle relaxing properties. Prone to cause tolerance, chronic users of benzodiazepines are at a greater risk of suffering from many side effects, which include dizziness, lightheadedness, impaired thinking and judgment, memory loss, nausea, stomach upset, and blurred or double vision.

Examples of drugs in this category: Alprazolam (Xanax), chlordiazepoxide (Librium), clonazepam (Klonopin), diazepam (Valium), flurazepam (Dalmane), lorazepam (Ativan), midazolam (Versed), quazepam (Doral), temazepam (Restoril) and triazolam (Halcion)

2) Cholesterol lowering drugs: Statins can lower blood levels of cholesterol, which in turn can impair memory as well as other mental processes. As discussed earlier, fats and lipids are essential for the nervous system, and their reduction can lead to adverse cognitive effects. It is also important to note that there is a long list of other possible side effects of statins.

   Examples of drugs in this category: Atorvastatin (Lipitor), fluvastatin (Lescol), lovastatin (Mevacor), pravastatin (Pravachol), rosuvastatin (Crestor) and simvastatin (Zocor).

3) Hypertension drugs: Beta-blockers function by reducing the heart rate and lowering blood pressure. Side effects can include dizziness, insomnia, fatigue, loss of sex drive, depression, and digestive disorders.

   Examples of hypertensive drugs: Atenolol (Tenormin), carvedilol (Coreg), metoprolol (Lopressor, Toprol), propranolol (Inderal), sotalol (Betapace), timolol (Timoptic).

If you are currently taking any of the above-mentioned medications, you may want to consult with your physician regarding their side effects, and the side effects of the side effects. For example, insomnia in itself can cause brain deterioration.

A healthy body equals a healthy brain

Many health conditions can be prevented, eliminated, or the symptoms significantly reduced through exercise. Indeed, conditions such as diabetes, cardiovascular disease, osteoporosis, and depression respond quite well to exercise. One of the major effects of exercise is that it improves blood flow and oxygen delivery to your entire body including your brain, which of course helps it to function optimally.

Numerous studies confirm the benefits of exercise for brain health and memory. Interestingly, a study conducted at the University of Pittsburgh also shows that older adults who engaged in physical activity (walking) lost less gray matter than those who did not. The research also suggests that participation in exercise earlier in life might be predictive of less cortical shrinkage in late adulthood. The nine-year follow up also showed that active individuals had a lesser risk of dementia.[1]

Numerous studies confirm the benefits of exercise for brain health and memory.

Chapter five will discuss the impact of exercise in detail and offer suggestions for making it a part of your life.

Chronic stress and mental aging

Stress can have a direct impact on all parts of your body, from digestion to muscles, to the immune system, as well as your brain. Stress has been shown to affect short-term memory, and recent scientific studies are showing that even mild stress can, over time, alter brain chemistry. While we all experience stress from time to time, it is high stress levels experienced over time that cause the most damage, and can possibly lead to Alzheimer's or early-onset dementia, depending on the body's response to the stressors and its ability to adapt.

As mentioned earlier, myelin is responsible for signal transmission through nerve cells in the brain and is produced by cells known as oligodendrocytes. Interestingly, chronic stress increases the number of oligodendrocytes. Recent studies show that being subjected to chronic stress generates more oligodendrocytes and less neurons than normal. The resulting excess of myelin in some areas of the brain can disrupt the lines of communication within the brain.

Chapter six will take an in-depth look at the impact of stress on your brain and provide you with tools to deal with stress.

Social aspects and your brain

Maintaining full, meaningful relationships and social interaction is a fundamental ingredient for cognitive sharpness. Many social experiments and reports have shown that a weak social support network is associated with chronic depression. And, not surprisingly, many studies also show a direct connection between brain health and social connectedness as we age.

We humans are social creatures: just as we have a need for food and shelter, social relationships are very important. A famous experiment conducted on couples illustrates this further. A man and woman were brought into a lab, and the woman was connected to a brain scanner, while her significant other remained in a chair close next to her. At random times, the husband would receive a painful electrical shock. The woman, who knew when her partner was going to get shocked, was instructed to either hold his hand or to hold onto a small object. After scanning her brain activity, they found that her reward system (part of the brain that gets engaged

Just as we have a need for food and shelter, social relationships are very important.

when we are happy and rewarded) was active when she was holding his hand, both when he was being shocked and when he wasn't in pain—but it was most active when she held his hand as he was being shocked. Holding your partner's hand feels nice, but it's particularly meaningful when you know that he needs your love and affection.

Interestingly, a study published in the *Scientific American* showed that through social interactions, youth can pass some of their stamina on to the elderly, refining the older generation's cognitive capacities and vascular health and also elongating their life span. Research was conducted on fruit flies that had a specific mutation in their DNA that coded for the Sod1 enzyme, usually associated with Alzheimer's disease in humans. These mutated fruit flies lived almost twice as long when they were kept in the presence of young, energetic flies rather than by themselves.[2]

Does genetics play a role in aging?

Basic biology has taught us that the action of one single nucleotide sequence (nucleotides are building blocks of DNA and RNA and the sequence refers to how they are ordered) can be detrimental on the human body. In animal experiments, remarkable effects were found when a gene was altered or deleted.

Scientists are explaining that aging is not a simple "wear and tear" of our bodies. The deterioration of our bodies is only the result of a lack of replacements. All components in our body, like teeth, bone, and skin can age, but the inefficient maintenance or replacement of them is what triggers the signs of aging. Others still refute this theory by quoting the findings of one veterinary nutritionist, Clive McCay. McCay and his team were the first to prove that a caloric restricted diet can slow aging in controlled animal subjects.

Recent science has also proven that the connection between intelligence and speed-of-information processing/brain function is due to a common gene or set of genes in gene-hunting studies for IQ.[3] Detecting these genetic factors will aid in identifying mechanisms that confer individuals with resilience to endure the inevitable age-related variations in neural architecture and function.

An isolated gene in mice, called the Nogo Receptor 1, was the first real step forward into the genetic control of brain aging. This gene is liable for shutting down neuronal plasticity once a mouse reaches adulthood. After blocking it in old mice, their brains became malleable again, just like when they were young. Ever noticed that kids and adolescents can learn a new language quicker than an adult? That's the work of the Nogo Receptor 1. Learn more about how our brains age and the role of genetics in the next chapter.

---

[1] Erickson KI, Raji CA, Lopez OL, Becker JT, Rosano C, Newman AB, et al. "Physical activity predicts gray matter volume in late adulthood: The cardiovascular health study." *Neurology*, (October 13, 2010).

[2] Woodruff-Pak, Diana S. "Animal models of Alzheimer's disease: therapeutic implications." *Journal of Alzheimer's Disease* 15.4 (2008): 507-521.

[3] de Geus, E.J., Genet, Boomsma Behay, Martin, N.G., & Wright, M.J. "Genetics of brain function and cognition," 31(6): 489–495 (November 2001).

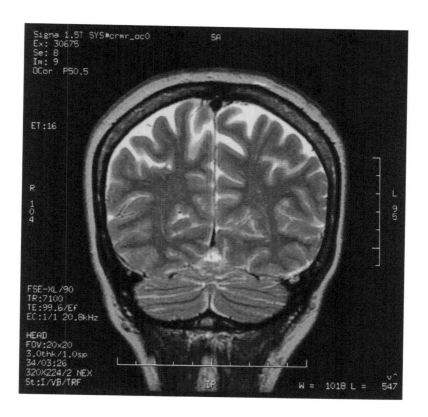

Signa 1.5T SYS#crmr_oc0   SA
Ex: 30675
Se: 8
Im: 9
OCor P50.5

ET:16

R
1
0
4

L
9
5

FSE-XL/90
TR:7100
TE:99.6/Ef
EC:1/1 20.8kHz

HEAD
FOV:20x20
3.0thk/1.0sp
34/03:26
320X224/2 NEX
St:I/VB/TRF   IP   W = 1018 L = 547

Chapter 2

A LOOK INSIDE

HOW OUR BRAINS AGE

Science has begun to understand the mechanisms of the aging brain.

Sooner or later, most of us start to feel the slow process of aging. Whether it is in your muscles when you exercise or a new found joint pain you have in the mornings, the effects of aging can be felt everywhere in the body. However, this aging process may be most noticeable in the brain. Brain aging is often linked to cognitive decline as well as dementia. Cognitive decline presents itself clinically through the deterioration of short-term and long-term memory and in a declining ability to do simple mental tasks. That is why understanding the genetic and physiological processes that take place in the brain is important to scientists and doctors who are looking for ways to slow down or reverse this negative impact of aging.

Recently, science has begun to understand the mechanisms of the aging brain and define what happens in the most complex structure of the human body as it ages. Researchers are identifying various biochemical players such as genes and proteins, as well as certain structures within the brain that are affected as we age, and they are looking at what can be done medically to treat the cognitive decline that is often associated with aging.

Cognitive decline that comes from aging varies greatly from individual to individual. Some people experience severe memory loss and dementia early into the aging process, while others experience almost no decline in mental acuity even as they get older. It wasn't until recently that scientists could begin to understand what actually resulted in these differences. Two recent scientific studies have shown that genetics may be accountable for some of these inconsistencies.[1] Scientists have discovered many different genetic markers and genes that may have an impact on declining cognitive ability. For instance, when a gene called apolipoprotein E is overexpressed in humans, there is a link to amyloid plaque formation in the brain, and thus, Alzheimer's disease and early-onset dementia. Overexpression, in this case, simply means that a gene is making more protein than usual in a typical individual.

The presence of another gene can affect the output of brain-derived neurotrophic factor (BDNF) which is a protein produced in the brain that is responsible for the maintenance and growth of neurons and synapses. Neurons and synapses in the brain are structures that are required for learning and memory. A neuron is a cell that is responsible for communicating brain activity to other cells, and a synapse is the specific area where these cells connect to other cells. Thus, having genes that produce more BDNF has been linked to greater levels of cognitive function.

Two other genes produce a protein called kidney and brain expressed protein, referred to as KIBRA, as well as a protein called calsyntenin. When these two proteins work in tandem, they can boost memory and cognitive functioning in humans. The research shows that genes and the amount of expression levels of certain proteins can greatly influence memory. Different expression levels of these genes in people can cause various and inconsistent cognitive results. However, why is it that these effects are more prevalent as someone ages? The answer may lie in a theory known as the "resource modulation hypothesis."

The resource modulation hypothesis states that losses in neurochemical and structural brain resources, such as neurons and synapses, associated with normal aging create a situation where these genetic differences more greatly affect the older generation rather than the developing brain in adolescents.[2] For instance, a lower amount of expressed BDNF in young adults may not affect their memory because their brains are still functioning with maximum resources. As the brain gets older and as structures such as neurons and synapses degrade or die, the effect of low amounts of BDNF may have a higher impact on memory since the brain has less resources to devote to memory retention.

Genetic makeup *has a greater effect on cognitive function as someone ages than it does when the subject is still young.*

It is important to note that this is a working theory, and much more research needs to be done to fully understand the role genetics play in the aging brain. However, it is becoming increasingly apparent that different genetic makeup has a greater effect on cognitive function as someone ages than it does when the subject is still young.

The implications of having certain biomarkers that may be able to predict cognitive deterioration are huge. Doctors, one day, may be able to test for certain genes and be able to determine treatment or preventative care for a patient regarding the decline of cognitive function as a result of aging.

Recent studies have also shown that a specific regulatory gene, which is a gene that regulates or controls the expression of another gene and its protein products, plays a part in the physiological processes of the aging brain. A gene regulator named REST, or RE1-silencing Transcription Factor, is very active in the fetal brain but is then switched off during the first few months after birth. It has been discovered that in some individuals, REST switches back on as the brain ages.[3] The switching back of REST to on is extremely important for the aging brain, as it helps protect against the degradation of neurons in critical brain regions as well as protecting these neurons from toxic effects caused by other abnormal proteins.

REST also turns off genes that promote other types of brain cell death. In the study, mice were genetically engineered to not express REST in their brains. The mice developed fine through adolescence and into adulthood. However, when the mice started to age past that, they began to have cognitive problems. After examining their brains post-mortem, scientists discovered that there was a significant amount of neuron death in the cortex and hippocampus compared to normal, healthy mice. The cortex and hippocampus are also the same places where most neurological death occurs in those afflicted with Alzheimer's disease.

This study was then replicated in research worms called C. elegans. The scientists discovered that REST was necessary in these worms for the maintenance of cognitive function as the worms aged. This showed that REST is important across species.

Further experiments were conducted to show how the mechanism REST is different in various groups of people. Subjects with cognitive decline and early onset dementia were shown to have a correlation with a decrease in REST. As REST expression decreased, so did cognitive function. Cell culture experiments revealed why that may be the case. The proposed mechanism involves stressed neurons communicating with each other to produce REST in the cytoplasm. Cytoplasm is the liquid substance that resides in the cell that is contained by the cellular membrane. REST must then travel to the nucleus of the cell to function properly. However, in patients that had Alzheimer's disease, REST never made it to the nucleus. It was engulfed and destroyed by the cell, much like a mutated protein would be.

The researchers then looked at the brain cells of those afflicted with other types of memory loss and dementia. It was found that these types of cognitive impairment also had cells showing a misplaced REST protein. This discovery is very important going forward. If scientists can figure out a way to reroute REST back to the nucleus of the cell, they may be able to stave off some of the negative impacts of an aging brain.

Another difference between the aging brain and the young brain is plasticity. A young brain is much more adaptable, allowing for learning and quicker recovery from brain injury. The aging brain is much more rigid than the young brain, and the connections between neurons are slower in an older brain. This is part of the reason that the aging brain starts to see cognitive decline.

A recent scientific study has shown a possible mechanism for these differences.[4] Researchers spent several months studying the synaptic connections of mice from their younger days into adulthood. They discovered that there is a switch in the brains of these mice that essentially represses the plasticity of the aging brain called the Nogo Receptor 1 gene (mentioned earlier). When this gene was overexpressed in younger mice, it resulted in a significant decrease of brain plasticity, and, similarly, when the gene was knocked out in older mice, they showed plasticity levels of younger mice.

Mice were then studied to see if the gene could be manipulated for recovery after a traumatic injury. Old mice that had a decreased expression of the Nogo Receptor 1 gene were able to relearn complex motor tasks much faster than their normal expression counterparts. Interestingly, their level of recovery was similar to the recovery speed of younger mice. This is extremely promising for the treatment of humans who have had a stroke or other serious brain injury as patients are often required to relearn fine motor movements such as writing and talking. Manipulation of the Nogo Receptor 1 gene could lead to different types of therapies for older populations recovering from these injuries.

Of course, other molecules have been implicated in brain aging. A study done by researchers at the Albert Einstein School of Medicine investigated a molecule referred to as NF-κB.[5] This molecule plays a role in DNA replication and the body's inflammatory response. By investigating the levels of NF-κB in mice at various stages of life, they discovered that the expression of this molecule increases in the hypothalamus of mice brains as they age.

Researchers performed cognitive tests on older adult mice with normal levels of NF-κB as well as those that had been genetically engineered to have brain levels of NF-κB that were similar to young mice. The mice that had the inhibition performed far better on cognitive tests, such as water mazes, than those that had normal aging brain levels of NF-κB. This may be because of the inflammatory properties of NF-κB. If NF-κB is reduced in the brain, there might be less of a loss of brain tissue resulting in a healthier, more efficient brain. This research again shows promising results in terms of treatment for the aging brain through the manipulation of the expression of NF-κB to treat brain-related cognitive decline.

Recent scientific research is also showing that a fundamental structure that is on all chromosomal DNA can be a good indicator of cognitive decline and brain age.[6] This structure is called a telomere, which is simply the end region of DNA that contains no important gene or coding information. This is essential for a strand of DNA because when the repli-

*The shortening of **telomere length**, specifically in the cells of the hippocampus of the brain, has been linked to diminishing brain volume.*

cation of DNA occurs, the process cannot biologically continue all the way to the very end of the chromosome. Thus, when DNA is replicated, each chromosome is slightly shorter than the chromosome it was copied from. The telomere is extremely important as it makes sure no valuable DNA is lost. A malfunctioning telomere system can lead to cancer. Shortening telomeres can also trigger apoptosis, which is a cell-programmed death triggered by various conditions in the body's environment. In this case, apoptosis can be initiated to prevent cells with not enough telomere buffers from replicating. This is a desired safety mechanism because cells that replicate without the proper telomere buffer will not function properly.

The shortening of telomere length, specifically in the cells of the hippocampus of the brain, has been linked to diminishing brain volume. It has also been suggested that people with shorter telomeres are at a greater risk for devastating neurological diseases over time, such as Alzheimer's disease. The mechanism for this result is believed to be that shorter telomere length allows a cell to replicate less before it eventually dies. If a cell has short telomeres, it will deplete its necessary buffer of telomere much quicker than a cell with longer telomeres, resulting in less replication. This decrease in replication and increase in programmed cell death leads to a loss of brain mass and, thus, cognitive decline. This telomere shortening is more prevalent as you get older, and cells have reproduced to their capacity.

When telomeres get too short, the cell will trigger its cell death, and the cell will no longer be able to reproduce. It is important to note that this information is preliminary, and that more research needs to be done to fully understand what roles telomeres play in the aging brain and diminished brain health in older people.

Having a direct effect on telomeres is an enzyme called telomerase, which helps to rebuild and lengthen telomeres. Interestingly, there is direct correlation between telomerase activity and psychological well-being, physical health, and longevity. In a study performed at U.C. Davis, researchers discovered that meditation directly affects a person's psychological well-being, which, in turn, affects "telomerase" in immune cells.[7]

An increased focus of research in the past few years has led to a wealth of new information and discoveries about our aging brains. Whether it is the interaction of different hormones in the brain or the discovery of new receptors such as Nogo 1, each new piece of information is allowing scientists to shed more light on the complexity of the brain. Moving forward, scientists will use these discoveries as the basis for further therapies and treatments. Scientists and doctors may also use the information as markers to determine the likelihood that someone is vulnerable to diseases and conditions related to diminishing brain activity. In turn, those individuals can take a corrective course of action, such as monitoring diet or starting a specific treatment protocol.

[1] Vitelli, Romeo. "Genetics and the Aging Brain." *Psychology Today*, (May 20, 2013). http://www.psychologytoday.com/blog/media-spotlight/201305/genetics-and-the-aging-brain.

[2] Backman, Lars, Chicherio, C., Heekeren, H., Lindenberger, U., Nagel, I., Shu-Chen, L. "Age-Related Decline in Brain Resources Modulates Genetic Effects on Cognitive Functioning." *Frontiers in Neuroscience.* 2.2 (2008) http://www.ncbi.nlm.nih.gov/pmc/articles/PMC2622748/

[3] Dutchen, Stephanie. "The Aging Brain Needs REST." *Harvard Medical School News* (March 19, 2014). http://hms.harvard.edu/news/aging-brain-needs-rest-3-19-14.

[4] Hathaway, Bill. "Flip of a single molecular switch makes an old brain young." Yale News (March 6, 2013). http://news.yale.edu/2013/03/06/flip-single-molecular-switch-makes-old-brain-young.

[5] Winter, Caroline. "Scientists Discover a Brain Region That Controls Aging." *Bloomberg Businessweek* (May 2, 2013). http://mobile.businessweek.com/articles/2013-05-02/scientists-discover-a-brain-regionthat-controls-aging.

[6] Rasgon, Natalie. "Cells' protective DNA linked to size of brain region vital for memory." *Stanford Medicine News Center* (July 22, 2014). http://med.stanford.edu/news/all-news/2014/07/cells_-protective-dna-linked-to-size-of-brain-region-vital-for-m.html.

[7] "Research Is In: Meditation Is Good For Cellular Health." *UC Davis News and Research.* http://www.ls.ucdavis.edu/dss/news-and-research/shamatha-project-nov10.html.

Chapter 3

FOOD FOR THOUGHT

HOW DIET AFFECTS BRAIN HEALTH

*Even something as simple as a **lack** of **vitamin B1** can cause serious damage to the thalamus and hypothalamus.*

Perhaps, one of the most important and most controllable factors in brain health is your diet. What you ingest can either support or destroy cells. It is important to realize that you can lose millions of brain cells every day due to poor eating habits and lack of proper nutrition. But it is also possible to grow new cells, neurons, and synapses once nutritional needs are met. And when this happens, you will notice a corresponding rise in mental performance and feel better across the board.

Choosing foods that have a positive rather than a negative impact on your brain takes a conscious effort, but it's not difficult. Asking your brain to continue running at its optimal potential without giving it the nutritional support it needs is like asking your car to run without oil. Eventually, parts will wear out, and the car won't run. The origin of many brain disorders, outside of infection, genetics, and trauma, is predominantly dietary.[1-2] Even something as simple as a lack of vitamin B1 can cause serious damage to the thalamus and hypothalamus, resulting in loss of mental activity and, in severe cases, lead to coma and death.

How certain foods or lack of certain nutrients negatively impacts your brain will give you an important understanding about which foods to limit or avoid and which are vital for brain health.

Alcohol: Even small amounts of alcohol can cause damage to cells in the part of the brain responsible for memory and cognition. Alcohol is considered poison to the brain, so even if you're doing everything else right, alcohol will cause a decline in cognitive function and can significantly deplete thiamine (vitamin B1) levels.[3]

Dehydration: Simple as it may be, not getting enough water can cause your brain or mind to get "fuzzy," confused, and slow. "The thirst mechanism slows down as you age, so you might not always be aware that you might need water. One of the symptoms of dehydration is mental confusion" (Susan A. Nitzke, R.D., Ph. D., University of Wisconsin, Dept. of Nutritional Sciences).

Even mild dehydration can affect energy level, mood, and your ability to think clearly. Mild dehydration begins when there is just a 1–2 percent loss in the normal water volume of the body, at which point, the effects are already beginning to take place. Remember, thirst is not the first indicator of your need to hydrate. In tests involving young men and women, mild dehydration caused headaches, fatigue, difficulty concentrating and performing mental tasks, tension, and anxiety. Female subjects exhibited adverse changes in mood that were substantially greater than male subjects.[4]

B vitamins: The B vitamins are the most important essential nutrients for helping to keep your mind sharp. Your body uses B vitamins to turn food into mental energy and to manufacture and repair brain tissue, so deficiencies in thiamin, niacin, vitamin B6, and B12 can all cause mental dysfunction. Low levels of boron have been shown to contribute to a decrease in electrical activity in the brain as well as impaired hand-eye coordination, which require explicit signals from the brain.[5]

A 2005 study published in the *American Journal of Clinical Nutrition* found that high levels of homocysteine and low levels of folate (folic acid), vitamin B6, and vitamin B12 indicated an increased risk of cognitive decline.[7] People who consumed at least 400 micrograms of folate had a 50 percent lower risk of Alzheimer's. Poultry, sweet potatoes, black eyed peas, and lentils are all good sources of B vitamins. You can also consider a supplement of B vitamins.

Sugar: High glycemic foods cause sugar surges in the blood, and few foods produce as much of a surge in blood glucose as those made with refined flour and sugar.[2] Foods that are easily and quickly digested saturate the bloodstream with glucose and stimulate a surge in insulin, all of which causes inflammation and cellular destruction. The brain has no pain receptors, so we can't feel inflammation in the brain the way we can with arthritis or an injury to the body.

Eat for Your Brain

Antioxidants: Pomegranates, grapes, citrus, and berries of all kinds are loaded with antioxidants, with blueberries at the top of the research list for their affect on cognitive function.[6] Antioxidants protect cells against oxidative stress, resulting in cell structure damage which can lead to cell degeneration. Add bilberries, raspberries, strawberries, blackberries, açai berries, gogi berries, and any other bright or dark skinned berry you can find to your diet.

Boron: Boron can help prevent the loss of calcium, and in this case, what's good for the bones is also good for the brain. In tests of memory, perception, and attention, people low in boron did not perform as well as those who had higher amounts of boron in their system. Researchers have found that reflexes and mental alertness improved when people were given additional boron. It doesn't take a lot: 1–3 milligrams can prevent the loss of calcium and keep the mind strong.[8] Dried fruits, nuts, dried beans, and green leafy vegetables are all good sources of boron.

Catechins: Catechins are a type of polyphenol which is a phytochemical, or chemical found in plants. According to research published in Volume 23 of the *European Journal of Neuroscience,* catechins show beneficial effects on amyloid protein deposits, one of the key factors associated with Alzheimer's.

In a study published in the journal of *Biochemical and Biophysical Research Communications,* researchers demonstrated for the first time that introducing an extremely low concentration of unfractionated green tea polyphenols and low concentrations of their active ingredient, epigallocatechin-3-gallate (EGCG), induced neurite outgrowth and increased the activity of a nerve growth factor known as brain-derived neurotrophic factor (BDNF).[9] A neurite is any projection from the cell body of a neuron, usually an axon or a dendrite. BDNF is essential for the growth, maintenance, and survival of neurons.

Cholesterol: We've been taught that cholesterol is bad, but the truth is that the body can't live without it. Cholesterol is necessary for the brain to thrive, and plays a fundamental role as a building block of cell membranes. It's important for brain-supporting elements such as vitamin D, and it's an essential fuel for establishing neuron-to-neuron connections.[10]

In a study reported in *The Journal of Geriatric Psychiatry* examining the effects of high cholesterol and memory in older adults, researchers concluded, "It is possible that individuals who survived beyond age eighty-five, especially those with high cholesterol, may be more robust (with regard to memory function)."[11] Only animal products contain cholesterol, and your body can make its own, so sticking to a varied diet that includes pastured meats, eggs, dairy, and wild seafood is best for most people.

Coffee: Caffeine has been shown to improve mental functioning because it dilates blood vessels, thereby allowing more blood flow to the brain. It's great in a pinch, but the downside is that the buzz wears off in about six hours. According to Suzette Evans, Ph.D., an assistant professor at Columbia University College of Physicians and Surgeons and the New York State Psychiatric Institute, "People who drink one or two cups of coffee can definitely have improved mental performance. But if you drink it all the time and throughout the day, you'll build up a tolerance to the stuff and won't get the same benefits. Too much can be dehydrating and can make you jittery, reducing your concentration."

Fats: Less than 100 years ago, the Standard American Diet didn't exist. Our ancestors consumed food in its natural state, complete with all the delicious fat. These fats protected them against diseases. So, when we talk about fats as being healthy, we're referring to natural fats found in pastured meat, eggs, wild fish and game, butter, full fat dairy, nuts, seeds, and avocados. Not hydrogenated and trans fats with molecularly changed structures like those found in baked snack foods, margarine, and other processed or "manufactured" foods.

Experts in the field of biochemistry have found that saturated fats constitute 50 percent of all cell membranes. Without it, calcium cannot be incorporated into the skeletal structure.[12] Remember, what's good for the bones is good for the brain. The brain is almost 60 percent fat. Essential fatty acids (EFAs), particularly Omega-3s, are among the molecules that are essential to brain neural-transmission and performance.[13]

And don't forget *plant oils*. According to research done by Jordan Rubin, N.M.D., Ph.D., and founder of Garden of Life whole food nutritional supplements, "One ounce of clove oil has the antioxidant capacity of 450 pounds of carrots, 120 quarts of blueberries, or 48 gallons of beet juice." Though it would be difficult to consume that much clove oil, you can use it in baking, soups, smoothies, or mix a bit with honey and spread it on sprouted grain bread (Caution: do not take clove oil straight – it will burn!). Olive, coconut, sesame, almond, peanut, sunflower, and avocado oils are among the plant oils that you can consume raw in salads and soups.

Macronutrients: Proteins, fats, and carbohydrates all have an effect on mental processes and the brain's ability to perform. In a test of paragraph recall and attention, test subjects showed improvements after being given drinks based on each macronutrient. Protein and fat proved to be as significant as energy enhancing carbs within the parameters of the test but did not cause the elevated blood glucose levels associated with carbohydrates.[14]

Once again, it is important to consider the source of our protein. Get it from pasture-raised animal meats, eggs, dairy, nuts, seeds, seafood, and dried beans. Stick with unrefined carbohydrates such as fruits, vegetables, and whole grains. Avoid refined flours and sugars since they produce spikes in blood sugar that cause inflammation.

Cognition Rehab

Hydrate: Staying properly hydrated is important for everyone, not just those who work out or participate in sports. Your body is made up of 60 percent water, and most experts agree that women need at least eight 8-ounce glasses of water per day and more if you are a man. You will also need more water if you are exercising, in a hot environment, at high altitude, pregnant, or have certain health conditions.

You can drink water straight or get it from fruits with high water content. Watermelon, strawberries, grapefruit, and cantaloupe have 90 percent or more water by volume. Peaches, pineapple, raspberries, oranges, blueberries, and plums have 85 percent or more. At the top of the list for vegetables are cucumbers, lettuce, zucchini, radishes, celery, and tomatoes with 94 percent or more. Broccoli, cauliflower, peppers, red cabbage, spinach, and eggplant come in at a healthy 90 percent or more.[15]

Starting your day with a fresh homemade fruit-ade is a good way to get your mental juices going. Simply add slices of lemon, lime, and orange to water and chill overnight. In the morning, down a cup of this refreshing and healthy drink to replace fluids lost overnight in the repair process.

Drink tea: In addition to being hydrating, green tea is one of the best sources of catechins along with cocoa and black tea to a lesser extent. Take a relaxing break and drink your green tea chilled or hot. Infuse it with fruit slices for a potent brain-boosting elixir.

Eat good fats: The unique metabolic needs of the brain can be affected with a single dose of MCTs (medium chain triglycerides), like those found in pure raw coconut oil. Remarkably, cognitive testing revealed that brief MCT treatment facilitated better performance on a cognitive assessment scale with improvement occurring almost immediately.[16]

Coconut oil stands up to high temperatures, so you can use it for all your cooking needs. Spread it over roasted chicken or use it in soups, stews, and smoothies. If you really love coconut, throw a dollop in your coffee. You won't taste it, but the fresh coconut aroma is a real treat.

Extra virgin olive oil is another good choice for brain health as it is high in antioxidants. Olive oil does not stand up to heat well, so be sure to use it for low temperature cooking and drizzling only.

Omega-3 fats, like those found in fish, may help to prevent age-related dementia as well as heart disease and lower your blood pressure.[17] Shoot for two servings a week but skip the fish that is high in mercury like tuna, swordfish, king mackerel, and marlin.

Be sure to avoid trans fats (found mostly in junk food), which have a host of known negative side effects on the body. In a landmark study performed by Dr. Gene Bowman of Oregon Health & Science

University showed, there is a direct correlation between high levels of trans fats in the blood and lower levels of cognitive functioning, as well as less total brain volume.

Don't skip meals: Breakfast supplies you with nutrients that have been depleted over the course of the previous day and throughout the night. Including small amounts of protein with each meal and getting about 30–40 percent of calories from healthy fats will give the brain what it needs to function well. Eating 4–5 smaller meals and drinking fluids in between is the best way to keep your system nourished and energized throughout the day.

Calorie restriction and intermittent fasting: You can find proponents on both sides of this fence, with some medical experts touting a myriad of health benefits including weight loss, detoxification, and the protection of brain cells. What's more, calorie restrictive diets appear to have an antiaging effect. On the other hand, many doctors are not so keen on the idea and focus more on healthy eating and exercise. Remember, if you fast you will lose weight quickly, and it most likely will come back quickly, too! If you are considering a fast or calorie restricted diet, it is best to discuss this with your physician and/or nutritionist.

1   Perlmutter, David, MD. *Grain Brain*. 1st Ed. New York: Little Brown and Company, 2013.

2   Pfrieger, Frank W. "The Surprising Role of Cholesterol in Brain Development." *Institute of Cellular and Integrative Neurosciences*, Université de Strasbourg (May 2014). http://www2.cnrs.fr/en/201.htm.

3   Vernon, Mark, MD. *Reversing Memory Loss*. 1st Ed. Boston: Houghton Mifflin, 1992.

4   Poitras, Colin. : UCONN Today, "Even Mild Dehydration Can Alter Mood." *UCONN Today* (February 2012). http://today.uconn.edu/blog/2012/02/even-mild-dehydration-can-alter-mood/.

5   "Boron Overview." *Life Extension Foundation for Longer Life* (2014). http://www.lef.org/abstracts/codex/boron_index.htm .

6   Rubin, Jordan S., NMD, PhD. *The Maker's Diet*. Lake Mary, Florida: Siloam, (2004).

7   Mooijiaart, Simon P, et al. "Homocysteine, vitamin B12, and folic acid, and the risk of cognitive decline in old age: The Leiden 85-plus study." *American Journal of Clinical Nutrition*, (2005). http://ajcn.nutrition.org/content/82/4/866.

8   Duke, James A. *The Green Pharmacy Guide to Healing Foods*. New York: Rodale, Inc., (2008).

9   Gunimeda, Usha, et al. "Green Tea Catechins." *Biochemical and Biophysical Research Communications*, 445.1, (2014). 218

10 224.http://www.sciencedirect.com/science/article/pii/S0006291X14002095

11 http://www.drperlmutter.com/brain-needs-cholesterol/

12 West, Rebecca , et al., "Better Memory Functioning Associated with Higher Total and Low-density Lipoprotein Cholesterol Levels." *American Journal of Geriatric Psychiatry* (September 2008): 781-85.

13 Enig, Mary G. and Fallon, Sally. *Nourishing Traditions: The Cookbook That Challenges Politically Correct Nutrition and the Diet Dictocrats*. 2nd Ed. Washington, DC: New Trends Publishing, Inc. (1999).

14 Cheng, Cy. "Essential Fatty Acids and the Human Brain." *U.S. National Library of Medicine National Institutes of Health* (2009). . http://www.ncbi.nlm.nih.gov/pubmed/20329590

[15] Kaplan, Randall J., et al. "Dietary Protein (and) Memory Performance." *American Journal of Clinical Nutrition* (2001). http://ajcn.nutrition.org/content/74/5/687.full.

[16] Kirschmann, John D. *Nutrition Almanac*. 7th Ed. Nutrition Search, Inc. New York: McGraw Hill (2007).

[17] Ji, Sayer. "MCT Fats Found in Coconut Oil." *GreenMedInfo* (2014). http://www.greenmedinfo.com/blog/mct-fats-found-coconut-oil-boost-brain-function-only-one-dose.

[18] Jacobsen, Maryann Tomovich. "What You Need to Know about Omega-3s." (May 2009). http://www.webmd.com/diet/features/omega-healthy-diet.

[19] "Wernicke-Korsakoff syndrome." *U.S. National Library of Medicine National Institutes of Health*, (May 2014). http://www.nlm.nih.gov/medlineplus/ency/article/000771.htm.

Chapter 4

A LITTLE EXTRA HELP

SUPPLEMENTS

This chapter provides a general overview of key supplements that may promote brain health and improve memory, especially for older individuals. Many people choose to include various dietary supplements in their healthcare routine to promote a better quality of life. But amid an abundance of different dietary supplements with varying claims about their safety and efficacy, it is important to make educated decisions about including supplements.

Dietary supplements often contain a variety of ingredients such as vitamins, minerals, herbs, amino acids, and other botanicals. Clinical research supports the usage of certain dietary supplements but not all. To ensure safe usage of any dietary supplements, first consult your healthcare provider and be sure to follow the label instructions. Please note that "natural" supplements are not always safe or effective; herbal supplements may contain other compounds and unknown ingredients.[1] Also, some dietary supplements may negatively interact with medications and/or pose additional risks for those with preexisting medical conditions.

Important note: Dosage for all supplements varies based on factors such as your age, gender, weight, and any preexisting medical conditions. Not all uses for the supplements listed in this chapter have been approved by the FDA. Long-

term, large-scale clinical studies are necessary to validate preliminary findings and suggestions. Supplements may interfere with prescribed or general medications. Adverse side effects may occur with use and/or high dosage. None of these supplements should be substituted for medications prescribed for you by your healthcare provider. Your healthcare provider can help you chose the best supplements and dosage for your specific condition and needs.

Alpha-Lipoic Acid

Overview:

Alpha-lipoic acid is a naturally occurring fatty acid, which helps cells generate energy by aiding in the metabolism of glucose.[2] This supplement is both fat- and water-soluble, allowing it to work throughout the body.

Health Function:

Because alpha-lipoic acid's diverse solubility allows it to pass easily into the brain, it may protect brain and nerve tissue. Researchers are investigating its potential as a treatment for stroke and other brain problems involving localized damage, such as dementia.[3] Alpha-lipoic acid is also involved in studies examining its potential role as an antioxidant, reducing the risk of chronic diseases such as diabetes mellitus and cataracts.[4] Antioxidants attack "free radicals," which are waste products created when the body turns food into energy. Free radicals can cause harmful chemical reactions and damage body cells, reducing the body's ability to fight infections. Their buildup can also damage organs and tissues.

Sources:

If you are healthy, your body likely makes enough alpha-lipoic acid. It is also found in red meat, organ meats (such as liver), and yeast. Additionally, alpha-lipoic acid supplements are available in capsule form. Your health care provider can also supply it by injection.[5]

Acetyl-L-carnitine

Overview:

Acetyl-L-carnitine is an amino acid (a protein component) naturally produced by the body, allowing it to convert fat into energy.[6]

Health Function:

Research suggests this supplement acts primarily as an antioxidant to neutralize free radicals and may reduce or prevent some of the damage they cause.

Several early studies indicate that acetyl-L-carnitine might slow the progression of Alzheimer's disease, relieve depression related to senility and other forms of dementia, and generally improve memory in the elderly. It may also improve thinking skills in people who have suffered a stroke.[7] Larger and better-designed studies, however, have not yet concluded any direct relation of acetyl-L-carnitine to improvement in these areas.[8]

Sources:
Food sources of acetyl-L-carnitine include red meat (especially lamb) and dairy products. It can also be found in lower amounts in fish, poultry, tempeh, wheat, asparagus, avocados, and peanut butter. Acetyl-L-carnitine is also available as a supplement and may be taken by prescription or given intravenously by a health care provider.[9]

Phosphatidylserine

Overview:
Phosphatidylserine is a key fatty acid and cell-membrane component involved in the maintenance of cellular function, especially within the brain.[10]

Health Functions:

Phosphatidylserine derived from cow brain may improve symptoms of Alzheimer's disease after 6 - 12 weeks of treatment. This treatment is apparently most effective in patients with less severe symptoms and may lose its effectiveness with extended use.[11] This supplement may also treat confusion in older individuals with senile dementia. Although phosphatidylserine made from cow brains can potentially improve attention, language skills, and memory in aging populations, it is not yet known whether newer products, which are taken from soy and cabbage, may have the same potential benefit.[12]

Sources:

The body can manufacture phosphatidylserine but meets most of its needs with foods such as soy, cow brain, and Atlantic mackerel.[13] Phosphatidylserine supplements are now commonly produced from cabbage or soy in response to concerns that earlier animal-sourced products could cause infections such as mad cow disease. Scientific research has utilized a dosage of 100mg of phosphatidylserine three times daily to combat Alzheimer's disease and other age-related cognitive impairment.[14]

Huperzine A

Overview:

Huperzine A is a highly purified alkaloid extract from a plant called Chinese club moss.

Health Functions:

The extract causes an increase in body levels of acetylcholine, which is one of the messenger-type chemicals used by our nerves to communicate in the brain, muscles, and other vital areas.[15] Huperzine A is primarily used to treat cognitive-function issues related to Alzheimer's disease, enhance memory and learning, and reduce age-related memory impairment. It is also utilized as a means of increasing alertness, improving energy, and protecting against nerve-damaging agents such as nerve gases.[16]

Sources:

For Alzheimer's disease symptoms specifically, huperzine A has been studied at oral dosages of 0.2 to 0.4 mg/day.[17] It is available as an oral supplement in capsule form but does not naturally occur in food sources.[18]

Vinpocetine

Overview:

Vinpocetine is synthesized from the alkaloid vincamine, which is extracted from periwinkle plant leaves.[19] It is chiefly suspected to increase blood flow to brain tissue.

Health Functions:

This supplement may enhance the delivery of oxygen and nutrients to the brain, as well as possibly prevent damage occurring from impaired nutrient delivery. Some research suggests that vinpocetine may also prevent the neurotoxic effects of Alzheimer's disease.[20] Vinpocetine is also used to prevent and reduce the chance of disability and death from ischemic (blood-clot caused) strokes.[21]

Sources:

Vinpocetine is synthetically derived as a supplement from a man-made chemical resembling a substance in the periwinkle plant.[22] Most clinical studies have used 10 mg of vinpocetine three times daily, taken orally or parentally, which means the drug is taken outside the digestive track.[23]

Antioxidants

Overview:

Antioxidants are chemicals that block the activity of harmful free radicals, which are highly reactive cellular waste products which can cause cell damage.[24]

Health Functions:

Consuming antioxidants can possibly lower your risk of developing cancer or neurological disease by minimizing the cell-damaging effects of oxidation (oxygen metabolism). Specifically, antioxidants can stop disease-causing chain reactions started by free radicals. Different types of antioxidants work either to prevent this harmful chain reaction or to stop it after it has started. [25]

Sources:

Some antioxidants are manufactured naturally by the body. Many fresh fruits and vegetables are also rich sources of other antioxidants. Types of dietary antioxidants include beta-carotene, lycopene, and vitamins A, C, and E.[26]

Flavonoids

Overview:

Flavonoids are a large family of compounds which are synthesized by plants from a common chemical structure.

Health Functions:

Many flavonoids appear to act like antioxidants by targeting and reducing damage from free radicals. It is not yet clear, however, how flavonoid consumption may impact older patients' risk of developing forms of neurodegenerative disease.[27]

Sources:

Many classes of fruits and vegetables serve as dietary sources of flavonoids, in addition to wine and tea.[28]

Alpha-GPC

Overview:

Alpha-GPC (alpha-glycerophosphocholine) is a medicinal chemical released from the breakdown of a fatty acid found in soy and other plants.[29]

Health Functions:

Clinical research suggests alpha-GPC increases a signaling chemical in the brain called acetylcholine, which is involved in communication for memory processes and learning functions. As a result, alpha-GPC is generally used for improving memory, thinking skills, and learning.[30] Additionally, this supplement might be involved in reducing the rate of cognitive decline when taken at high doses (1,000 to 1,200 mg per day) for mild to moderate Alzheimer's disease in combination with standard therapy (acetylcholinesterase inhibitors).[31]

Sources:

Alpha-GPC is commonly found as a natural constituent of red meat and organ tissue but is scarce in appreciable amounts in these naturally occurring sources. Most supplements are made synthetically via enzymatic creation from egg or soy lecithin.[32]

DHA

Overview:

DHA (docosahexaenoic acid) is a fatty acid which serves as a key structural component of the cerebral cortex.[33]

Health Functions:

DHA serves a prominent function in eye- and nerve-tissue development. It may also reduce the risk of heart and circulatory disease by decreasing the thickness of the blood and lowering blood triglyceride levels.[34] DHA is also required for the maintenance of normal brain function in adults. Plentiful DHA in the diet has been shown to improve learning ability and may potentially slow the progression of Alzheimer's disease.[35]

Sources:

This supplement most commonly occurs in algae, as well as in meat and oil from cold-water fish like mackerel, herring, tuna, halibut, salmon, and cod liver. Fish oil oral supplements are also available, and a typical dose contains 1,200 mg of fish oil with varying levels of DHA.[36] Researchers advise reading supplement labels to check levels of DHA, as this is not the same as the fish oil content.[37]

Zinc

Overview:

Zinc is an essential trace element for humans and is found in all parts of the body, particularly in muscles and bones.[38]

Health Functions:

Zinc is necessary for proper immune functioning. It is also involved in cell division, cell growth, wound healing, and the breakdown of carbohydrates.[39] Limited research suggests zinc supplements may also marginally slow the progression of symptoms in Alzheimer's disease.[40] Zinc plays a critical role in regulating neural communication, and, therefore, its intake could potentially affect memory formation and learning.[41]

Sources:

The major sources of zinc include high-protein foods, such as red meat, poultry, fish and seafood, whole cereals, and dairy products.[42] For adults, medical professionals utilize two standard dosages: a low dosage of 5–10mg, and a high dosage of 25–45mg. The low dose serves as a daily preventative, while the high dosage should be taken by those at risk for deficiency.[43]

Citicoline

Overview:

Citicoline is a naturally occurring human brain chemical in the form of an exogenous sodium salt.[44]

Health Function:

This supplement may potentially increase a brain chemical called phosphatidylcholine, which is important for brain function. Also, it appears to function as a stabilizer of cell membranes and reduces the presence of free radicals.[45] Citicoline may decrease brain-tissue damage after injury, and potentially may be effective for reducing age-related memory problems, assisting stroke recovery, and improving memory and behavior in those with long-term blood-circulation problems in the brain.[46]

Sources:

Citicoline can be taken by mouth as a supplement, administered as a shot, or given intravenously. To potentially remedy decline in thinking skills as a result of aging, a dosage of 1,000–2,000 mg per day is suggested by researchers.[47]

Coenzyme Q10

Overview:

Coenzyme Q10 (CoQ10) is the only lipid-soluble antioxidant synthesized by our bodies.[48] CoQ10 levels decrease with age and may be especially low in those with cancer, diabetes, heart conditions, and Parkinson's disease.[49]

Health Functions:

This supplement is utilized by cells to produce energy for cell growth and maintenance. It also functions as an antioxidant, protecting the body from free-radical damage.[50] CoQ10 may also be effective for treating inherited or acquired disorders which limit cellular energy production, as well as for reducing high blood pressure. It may potentially slow decline in those with early Parkinson's disease, but it does not appear to be effective for treating the mid-stage of the disease.[51]

Sources:

CoQ10 levels are naturally high in organ meats such as heart, liver, and kidney, as well as in beef, soy oil, sardines, mackerel, and peanuts. Research studies have utilized CoQ10 doses in adults ranging from 50 mg to 1,200 mg, sometimes separated into several doses over a day.[52]

Ginseng

Overview:

Ginseng comes from any of 11 species of short, slow-growing perennial plants with fleshy roots.

Health Functions:

Early evidence suggests ginseng might temporarily and moderately improve cognitive functions like concentration and learning. It may also aid in fatigue prevention and energy stimulation, although these functions are not yet well documented.[53]

Sources:

Ginseng's active ingredient (ginsenosides) is only found in its natural root. Asian ginseng is considered more stimulating than American varieties. Standard doses of ginseng have not been established for treating any condition.[54]

Gotu kola

Overview:

Gotu kola is a perennial member of the parsley family with no taste or smell. Its leaf and stem components are used as medicinal supplements.[55]

Health Functions:

Several small studies suggest gotu kola may help reduce swelling and improve blood flow. As a result, this supplement may also increase collagen production to assist wound healing.[56] Additionally, gotu kola is reported to aid intelligence and memory when used as a brain tonic, but these results have yet to be verified in clinical research.[57]

Sources:

Gotu kola is available in capsules, eye drops, powder, extracts, and ointments. Dried gotu kola can also be made into a tea.[58]

Yerba mate

Overview:

Yerba mate is made from the naturally caffeinated leaves of the South American rainforest holly tree.[59]

Health Functions:

Yerba mate contains caffeine and other chemicals that stimulate the brain, heart, and muscles lining blood vessels.[60] As a result, it may potentially increase nutrient and oxygen supply to the heart, improve mood, and increase mental energy and focus.[61]

Sources:

Yerba mate is primarily consumed by drinking it as a tea infusion, simply called mate.

St. John's Wort

Overview:

St. John's wort is a flowering, weed-like herb with anti-inflammatory properties.[62]

Health Functions:

This supplement is thought to balance specific brain chemicals, thereby improving mood by acting on essential chemical messengers in the nervous system.[63] Additional research studies suggest that St. John's wort may be helpful in treating mild to moderate depression.[64]

Sources:

The plant's flowers and leaves are used to make capsules, tablets, tinctures, teas, and oil-based skin lotions.[65] For treating depression symptoms, the standard dose for adults is 300 mg of St. John's wort three times a day.[66]

Ginkgo

Overview:

The ginkgo plant is one of the longest-living tree species in the world. Herb-like ginkgo leaves are generally used to make medicinal extracts, although some supplements are manufactured from ginkgo seeds instead.[67]

Health Functions:

Current research suggests ginkgo may improve blood circulation, possibly enabling the brain, eyes, ears, and legs to function better. Additionally, it may slow the progression of Alzheimer's disease by interfering with changes in the brain that could negatively alter thinking.[68]

Sources:

Ginkgo is generally available as oral capsules, liquid soft-gels, tea extracts, and liquid extracts.[69] For dementia syndromes, a daily dosage of 120–240 mg of ginkgo leaf extract is recommended, divided into two or three doses.[70]

Maca

Overview:

Maca is a cultivated Peruvian root vegetable and a relative of the radish. It generally demonstrates a butterscotch-like odor.[71]

Health Functions:

This supplement may potentially act as an aphrodisiac in men, improve memory and energy levels, and reduce anxiety, but these results are currently inconclusive and lack clinical validation.[72]

Sources:

Maca is commercially available in several forms: capsules, powder, liquid, and tablets.[73] It is also prepared in foods by being baked, roasted, fermented, or as soup.[74]

Rosemary

Overview:

Rosemary is a small, shrub-like member of the evergreen family with a distinctive savory taste and scent.

Health Functions:

Although its mechanism is currently unclear, applying rosemary topically can stimulate the skin and increase blood circulation.[75] Evidence is currently inconclusive for its use as a remedy for age-related mental decline as high doses have had the opposite effect on this condition.[76]

Sources:

Rosemary leaf and oil are widely used as cooking spices, especially in Mediterranean dishes; the oil is also used in beverages and can be applied topically.[77]

Peppermint

Overview:

Oil from the leaves and flowering tops of the peppermint plant possesses the active ingredients menthol and menthone.

Health Function:

Aromatherapists claim peppermint's scent may improve concentration, stimulate the mind and body, decrease inflammation, improve digestion, and relieve stomach pain.[78] Peppermint oil may also improve digestion and relieve intestinal ailments by alleviating spasms. Early clinical evidence suggests peppermint may slightly improve memory and performance in mental tasks, but the supplement does not appear to improve attention or speed of completing tasks.[79]

Sources:

Pure peppermint oil or a liquid extract containing the oil can be taken directly or swallowed in capsules. Peppermint is also available as a spray or inhalant for treating throat, mouth, nose, sinus, and lung ailments. The leaves are sometimes brewed as a tea.[80]

Bacopa monnieri

Overview:

Bacopa monnieri, commonly known as water hyssop, is a staple of Indian medicine. The plant's crushed leaves generally have a lemon-like scent.[81]

Health Functions:

This supplement may promote neural stimulation by enhancing the nervous system's communication rate. This is accomplished by increasing the growth of nerve endings.[82] *Bacopa monnieri* also operates as an antioxidant.

Sources:

Bacopa monnieri can be ingested in a leaf, tablet, capsule, or powder form. Its standard dose is 300mg, assuming the bacoside content (the active compound) comprises 55 percent of the extract weight.[83] Because it is fat soluble and requires a lipoid transporter to be absorbed, it should be taken with a meal.[84]

Green tea

Overview:

Green tea is made from unfermented tea leaves and reportedly contains the highest concentration of a powerful class of antioxidants called polyphenols.[85]

Health Functions:

The antioxidants in green tea can neutralize free radicals and, therefore, may reduce or prevent damaging results for cells. MRI activity (Magnetic Resonance Imaging) indicates that people who drank green tea ultimately possessed greater activity in working-memory brain regions. Green tea may also block the plaque formation linked to Alzheimer's disease.[86]

Sources:

Most green tea supplements are sold as dried leaf tea in capsule form. Liquid extracts made from the leaves and leaf buds are also available. Doses of green tea vary significantly but usually range from 1–10 cups per day. Common doses are based on typical consumption in Asian countries (about three cups daily, providing 240–320 mg of polyphenols).[87]

Rhodiola

Overview:

Rhodiola is a Scandinavian herb with medicinal roots and edible leaves.

Health Functions:

Rhodiola extracts may protect cells from damage, regulate heartbeat, and improve learning and memory. None of these potential effects, however, have been studied in humans at this time.[88] This supplement is also considered a potential adaptogen, which is a substance that helps the body adapt to and resist physical, chemical, or environmental stress.[89]

Sources:

The rhodiola herb is available in capsules or as an extract. Additionally, its young leaves are edible, as are the roots, shoots, and stems. The use of rhodiola to combat fatigue and stress generally involves dosages within the 288–680 mg range.[90]

Magnesium

Overview:

Magnesium is a mineral present in relatively large amounts in the body. It is involved in over 300 chemical reactions that help maintain healthy body processes.[91]

Health Functions:

Magnesium activates enzymes, contributes to energy production, and helps regulate calcium levels, as well as copper, zinc, potassium, vitamin D, and other vital nutrients.[92] Sufficient magnesium levels are, therefore, required for proper bone growth and maintenance. This mineral is also required for the functional maintenance of nerves and muscles. It may also potentially decrease the risk of stroke in men, although these results are preliminary.

Sources:

Whole grains, nuts, and green leafy vegetables are excellent food sources of magnesium. Oral supplements are also available.[93] The standard dosage range for magnesium supplementation is 200–400mg.[94] Intravenous or injected magnesium can treat conditions such as eclampsia during pregnancy and certain heart arrhythmias.[95]

Turmeric

Overview:

Turmeric commonly functions as the main spice in curry. Its warm, bitter taste is frequently used to flavor curry powders, mustards, and cheeses. The turmeric root is also frequently used to make medicine.[96]

Health Functions:

The chemicals contained in turmeric may potentially decrease swelling and resulting inflammation. Curcumin, an active component of turmeric, can also function as a powerful antioxidant by fighting free radicals to prevent cellular damage.[97] Curcumin may lower the levels of two inflammatory enzymes in the body and hinder platelets from clumping together to form blood clots.[98] Research does not support the use of turmeric in treating conditions like Alzheimer's disease as individuals with Alzheimer's disease taking curcumin daily for six months failed to demonstrate any measurable improvements in clinical study.[99]

Sources:

Turmeric's roots and bulbs are used in medicine and food. These components are generally boiled and dried, resulting in the familiar yellow powder. Turmeric is available as capsules, fluid extract, or tincture. Since bromelain may increase the absorption and anti-inflammatory effects of curcumin, it is generally combined with turmeric supplements.[100]

1   U.S. Dept. of Health & Human Services. (2014, June). NC-CAM: Using Dietary Supplements Wisely. Retrieved Nov. 13, 2014.

2   Drugs.com. (2011, Oct.). Alpha Lipoic Acid. Retrieved Nov. 13, 2014.

3   Ehrlich, S. (2011, Apr.). University of Maryland Medical Center: Alpha-lipoic acid. Retrieved Nov. 13, 2014.

4   Blake, J. (2012). Are There Other Important Nutrients? *Nutrition and You* (2nd ed., p. 262). San Francisco: Pearson Benjamin Cummings.

5   Ehrlich, S. (2011, Apr.). University of Maryland Medical Center: Alpha-lipoic acid. Retrieved Nov. 13, 2014.

6   Ehrlich, S. (2011, Mar.). University of Maryland Medical Center: Carnitine (L-carnitine). Retrieved Nov. 13, 2014.

7   RxList. (2009). Acetyl-L-Carnitine Effectiveness, Safety, and Drug Interactions. Retrieved Nov. 13, 2014.

8   Ehrlich, S. (2011, Mar.). University of Maryland Medical Center: Carnitine (L-carnitine). Retrieved Nov. 13, 2014.

9   *Ibid.*

10 Christie, W. (2013, Apr.). The AOCS Lipid Library: Phosphatidylserine; structure, occurrence, biochemistry and analysis. Retrieved Nov. 13, 2014.

11 WebMD. (2009). Phosphatidylserine. Retrieved Nov. 13, 2014.

12 *Ibid.*

13 Souci S., Fachmann E., Kraut H. (2008). Food Composition and Nutrition Tables. Stuttgart: Medpharm Scientific Publishers.

14 WebMD. (2009). Phosphatidylserine. Retrieved Nov. 17, 2014

15 WebMD. (2009). Huperzine A. Retrieved Nov. 13, 2014.

16 Drugs.com. (2009, Oct.). Huperzine A. Retrieved Nov. 13, 2014.

17 *Ibid.*

18 ALZ Forum. (2014). Huperzine A. Retrieved Nov. 13, 2014.

19 Drugs.com. (2009). Vinpocetine. Retrieved Nov. 13, 2014.

20 Goepp, J. (2006, February). Life Extension Magazine: Vinpocetine. Retrieved Nov. 13, 2014.

21 WebMD. (2009). Vinpocetine. Retrieved Nov. 13, 2014.

22 *Ibid.*

23 Drugs.com. (2009). Vinpocetine. Retrieved Nov. 13, 2014.

24 National Cancer Institute. (2014, Jan.). Antioxidants and Cancer Prevention. Retrieved Nov. 13, 2014.

25 Davis, J. (2006, Apr.). WebMD Feature: How Antioxidants Work. Retrieved Nov. 13, 2014

26 National Institutes of Health. (2014, Oct.). MedlinePlus: Antioxidants. Retrieved Nov. 13, 2014.

27 Higdon, J., Drake, V. (2008, June). Micronutrient Information Center: Flavenoids. Retrieved Nov. 14, 2014.

28 Yao, L., Jiang, Y., Shi, J., Tomás-Barberán, F., Datta, N., Singanusong, R., Chen, S. (2004). Flavonoids In Food And Their Health Benefits. *Plant Foods for Human Nutrition*, 113-122.

29 WebMD. (2009). Alpha-GCP. Retrieved Nov. 13, 2014.

30 *Ibid.*

31 Examine.com. (2013, July). Alpha-GPC. Retrieved Nov. 14, 2014.

32 *Ibid.*

33 WebMD. (2009). DHA (docosahexaenoic acid). Retrieved Nov. 13, 2014.

34 *Ibid.*

35 Horrocks, L., Yeo, Y. (1999). Health benefits of docosahexaenoic acid (DHA). *Pharmacological Research*, 211-225.

36 WebMD. (2009). DHA (docosahexaenoic acid). Retrieved Nov. 13, 2014.

37 Ehrlich, S. (2011, Apr.). University of Maryland Medical Center: Docosahexaenoic acid (DHA). Retrieved Nov. 17, 2014.

38 International Zinc Association. (2011). Zinc: Essential for Human Health. Retrieved Nov. 14, 2014.

39 National Institutes of Health. (2013, Feb.). MedlinePlus: Zinc in diet. Retrieved Nov. 13, 2014.

40 WebMD. (2009). Zinc. Retrieved Nov. 13, 2014.
41 Medical News Today. (2011, Oct.). Zinc Important For Learning And Memory. Retrieved Nov. 13, 2014.
42 International Zinc Association. (2011). Zinc: Essential for Human Health. Retrieved Nov. 13, 2014.
43 Examine.com. (2014, July). Zinc. Retrieved Nov. 17, 2014.
44 Fioravanti, M., Buckley, A. (2006, Sep.). Citicoline (Cognizin) in the treatment of cognitive impairment. *Journal of Clinical Interventions in Aging*, 247–251.
45 *Ibid.*
46 WebMD. (2009). Citicoline. Retrieved Nov. 13, 2014.
47 *Ibid.*
48 Stocker, R. (2002). Possible Health Benefits of Coenzyme Q10. Oregon State University: Linus Pauling Institute. Retrieved Nov. 12, 2014.
49 Mayo Clinic. (2013, Nov.). Coenzyme Q10. Retrieved Nov. 13, 2014.
50 WebMD Medical Reference. (2013, June). Coenzyme Q10 - Topic Overview. Retrieved Nov. 13, 2014.
51 National Institutes of Health. (2011, Oct.). MedlinePlus: Coenzyme Q-10. Retrieved Nov. 13, 2014.
52 WebMD Medical Reference. (2013, June). Coenzyme Q10 - Topic Overview. Retrieved Nov. 13, 2014.
53 National Institutes of Health. (2012, Dec.). Ginseng, Panax. Retrieved Nov. 13, 2014.
54 WebMD. (2013, Apr.). Ginseng Supplements. Retrieved Nov. 13, 2014.
55 Ehrlich, S. (2012, Dec.). University of Maryland Medical Center: Gotu kola. Retrieved Nov. 14, 2014.
56 WebMD. (2009). Gotu kola. Retrieved Nov. 14, 2014.
57 HerbWisdom.com. (2014). Gotu Kola (Centella Asiatica). Retrieved November 14, 2014
58 American Cancer Society. (2008, Nov.). Gotu Kola. Retrieved Nov. 14, 2014.
59 WebMD. (2009). Mate. Retrieved Nov. 14, 2014.
60 *Ibid.*
61 Guayaki Brand. (2014). Yerba Mate. Retrieved Nov. 14, 2014.
62 Ehrlich, S. (2011, May). University of Maryland Medical Center: St. John's wort. Retrieved Nov. 14, 2014.
63 Drugs.com. (2014, Sep.). St. John's wort. Retrieved Nov. 14, 2014.
64 Ehrlich, S. (2011, May). University of Maryland Medical Center: St. John's wort. Retrieved Nov. 14, 2014.

[65] National Institutes of Health. (2014, May). MedlinePlus: St. John's wort. Retrieved Nov. 14, 2014.

[66] WebMD. (2012, Dec.). St. John's wort. Retrieved Nov. 14, 2014.

[67] National Institutes of Health. (2014, July). MedlinePlus: Ginkgo. Retrieved Nov. 14, 2014.

[68] WebMD. (2009). Ginkgo. Retrieved Nov. 14, 2014.

[69] Medicine.net (2014, Sep.). Ginkgo biloba. Retrieved Nov. 14, 2014.

[70] National Institutes of Health. (2014, July). MedlinePlus: Ginkgo. Retrieved Nov. 14, 2014.

[71] WebMD. (2009). Maca. Retrieved Nov. 14, 2014.

[72] Drugs.com. (2014, Sep.). Maca. Retrieved Nov. 14, 2014.

[73] *Ibid.*

[74] WebMD. (2009). Maca. Retrieved Nov. 14, 2014.

[75] WebMD. (2009). Rosemary. Retrieved Nov. 14, 2014.

[76] *Ibid.*

[77] Ehrlich, S. (2011, Apr.). University of Maryland Medical Center: Rosemary. Retrieved Nov. 14, 2014.

[78] American Cancer Society. (2008, Nov.). Peppermint. Retrieved Nov. 14, 2014.

[79] National Institutes of Health. (2014, July). MedlinePlus: Peppermint. Retrieved Nov. 14, 2014.

[80] American Cancer Society. (2008, Nov.). Peppermint. Retrieved Nov. 14, 2014.

[81] Examine.com. (2013, May). Bacopa monnieri. Retrieved Nov. 14, 2014.

[82] *Ibid.*

[83] *Ibid.*

[84] Bacopa-Monnieri.com. (2014, Mar.). Bacopa Monnieri extract. Retrieved Nov. 14, 2014.

[85] Ehrlich, S. (2011, Oct.). University of Maryland Medical Center: Green tea. Retrieved Nov. 14, 2014.

[86] Scott, P. (2013, Sep.). WebMD Feature: Health Benefits of Green Tea. Retrieved Nov. 13, 2014

[87] *Ibid.*

[88] WebMD. (2009). Rhodiola. Retrieved Nov. 14, 2014.

[89] Examine.com. (2013, Oct.). Rhodiola Rosea. Retrieved Nov. 14, 2014.

[90] *Ibid.*

[91] WebMD. (2009). Magnesium. Retrieved Nov. 14, 2014.

[92] Ehrlich, S. (2011, June). University of Maryland Medical Center: Magnesium. Retrieved Nov. 14, 2014.

[93] WebMD. (2009). Magnesium. Retrieved Nov. 14, 2014.

94 Examine.com. (2014, Mar.). Magnesium. Retrieved Nov. 17, 2014.

95 Ehrlich, S. (2011, June). University of Maryland Medical Center: Magnesium. Retrieved Nov. 14, 2014.

96 WebMD. (2009). Turmeric. Retrieved Nov. 17, 2014.

97 Ehrlich, S. (2011, Oct.). University of Maryland Medical Center: Turmeric. Retrieved Nov. 17, 2014.

98 *Ibid.*

99 WebMD. (2009). Turmeric. Retrieved Nov. 17, 2014.

100 Ehrlich, S. (2011, Oct.). University of Maryland Medical Center: Turmeric. Retrieved Nov. 17, 2014.

Chapter 5

MOVE IT OR LOSE IT

EXERCISE AND BRAIN HEALTH

When most people start an exercise program and commit to getting into better shape, the primary goals are usually improving their aesthetic image–getting thinner, more toned, or more muscular, as well as to manage health factors such as blood pressure, bone health, or diabetes. And while these are definitely important benefits, exercise also provides a host of health benefits for your brain.

Regular exercise is now being considered one of the top ways to treat or prevent Alzheimer's disease, as noted in a study published in the *Journal of Alzheimer's Disease.*[1] Researchers had subjects participate in a 12-week exercise program, and once it was finished, subjects demonstrated less intense brain activation when performing various mental tasks. This shows their brains were better equipped to process those functions.

Additionally, regular exercise also improved their memory and word recall. If you find that you have trouble remembering things on a regular basis, exercise may just be a great solution!

Researchers have also discovered that a regular exercise program will make your brain more resilient in times of stress, just as it makes your body more resilient as well. The stronger your muscles and bones are, the better they will be able to stand up to the daily stressors of life. Likewise, the stronger your brain becomes from exercise, the less day-to-day stress will impact your brain and memory.

Most forms of exercise have shown to provide a positive impact on reducing or eliminating anxiety, depression, general moodiness, symptoms of stress, and insomnia. As indicated in the chapters on sleep and stress, these issues can and do influence brain health negatively.

How various forms of exercise influence brain health

Strength Training: This is one of the most beneficial forms of exercise for enhancing muscular strength, body composition, and bone strength. Whether you use dumbbells, barbells, weight machines, or your own body weight, performing some type of resistance exercise provides a host of antiaging benefits.

While resistance training helps to improve mood, many people report it's one of the best forms of exercise for releasing pent up energy and feelings of aggression or anger.

If you strength train at a high enough intensity level by reducing your rest periods, you'll also get a good burst of endorphins released from the brain, which have a positive feel-good effect on the body. This same response can also be seen when someone is doing endurance cardio sessions and is often termed the "runner's high."

Strength training can also help to improve your mind-body coordination as you'll become more attuned to focusing on contracting just a particular group of muscles as you execute an exercise pattern. Having good mind-body control is very helpful, whether you want to try out a new physical experience later in life, or to have the confidence of being able to enjoy your favorite activity, pick up the grandkids, or carry groceries in from the car.

Cardiovascular Training: Cardiovascular exercise helps improve brain health because it increases your heart rate, which means more blood and oxygen are going to get into the brain. As greater blood flow reaches the hippocampus, a key area of the brain associated with memory, improvements in item recall are demonstrated.

One key area of memory that is especially improved with regular exercise is spatial memory— your brain's ability to remember where objects are located in relationship to the rest of your body. For instance, you would use this function of your memory to remember where to drive on your morning route to work.

When adults who perform regular physical activity are taken for neuroimaging of their brain, they show a larger hippocampus area for spatial memory compared to those who don't exercise regularly. The more developed and advanced a particular brain area becomes, the more it will be able to execute related tasks.

Engaging in cardiovascular exercise also helps to improve brain plasticity levels by stimulating the growth of new connections between cells in cortical areas of the brain, according to research published in the *Proceedings of the National Academy of Sciences*.[2] Also associated with plasticity is an increased level of gene expression, which increases the generation of new neurons.

Blood flow to the brain from exercise increases the total volume of an area of the brain called the dentate gyrus, which is related to verbal learning ability, as well as overall memory capacity.

Regular cardiovascular exercise can also assist with brain rejuvenation as it can trigger the release of growth factors that can signal brain stem cells to convert into new neurons.

Keep in mind that when it comes to cardio-vascular training, more intense exercise variations will have a greater influence on endorphin release. By no means do you have to be performing at top intensities to see benefits. Even lower intensity aerobic exercise, such as a brisk walk, can provide significant benefits, making it something that almost everyone can include in their life.

Yoga and mind-body modalities: Other forms of exercise that have become very popular are mind-body practices like yoga, Pilates, or Tai Chi, which also offer tremendous benefits for brain health.

A study published in the *Journal of Alternative and Complimentary Medicine*[3] reported that when subjects participated in a yoga exercise class, their levels of the brain chemical messenger GABA increased, which helps to relieve feelings of depression and anxiety. The subjects showed an increase of 27 percent of GABA in their brain after just a single session but showed no increase in the levels after a reading session, which was the alternative treatment. This illustrates how quickly exercise can exert its effects on the health of your brain.

Mind-body modalities are also exquisite stress relievers, both for relieving stress and improving your ability to handle new stress. What's more, these exercise forms also require you to learn new ways to move your body, thereby stimulating and building neuromuscular pathways, which is good for your nervous system and your brain.

Exercise variations that require you to learn new skills, such as ballroom dancing or learning a new sport you've never played before, will prove to be better at enhancing cognitive function than performing a form of exercise that involves a movement pattern you've done time and time again, such as running.

Learning a new physical activity is going to place a greater demand on cognition, just as learning any new activity would, but with the addition of increased blood flow and heart rate, you double up on the benefits!

Developing an exercise program for maximum benefit

Now that you see the main ways in which exercise can benefit your brain health, here are some guidelines to help you create your own brain health exercise program.

Most importantly, start from where you are. By that, I mean if you have not exercised in a long time, or in a few years, be sure to begin with gentle exercise, such as walking, gentle yoga, or an easy bike ride for a while and then slowly start adding intensity. You might also want to consult with a qualified personal trainer and / or your doctor before starting.

Forget "no pain, no gain." That attitude will only result in a quick burn out or an injury, both of which will derail your program. An essential key in getting the benefits of exercise is doing it regularly. People who exercise regularly, stay with it because they have found activity they enjoy. So, make it fun, invite some friends, and enjoy yourself!

Ideally, it is best to combine various forms of exercise throughout the week, mixing up strength training, aerobic exercise, and mind-body modalities. But, keep in mind, the most important thing is to just do it! It is the regular practice of exercise over time that is going to give you the most results.

With that being said, if you want to get the most benefit for your brain from exercise, consider the following suggestions. Add one physical activity form that will have you 'thinking' as you do it. This means it's something that you have to learn, so that you are making new neural connections in the brain as you build those movement patterns into memory. This could be ballroom dancing, as mentioned above, a new aerobics class that requires rhythm and coordination, golf, skiing, tennis, or strength training exercises you have not done before.

You'll also want to add cardiovascular exercise as well. This will boost a continuous oxygen flow into the brain. This could be jogging, a brisk walk, swimming, biking, etc. Shoot for 30 plus minutes, 2–3 times a week or more.

If you are of the fitness level to do it, add one or two higher intensity interval training sessions. This is the form of exercise that is going to best enhance the release of endorphins, providing mood-boosting benefits. In addition to that, the memory-boosting benefits of cardiovascular exercise will be most pronounced during this level of intensity.

A third component to add to your fitness regime is strength training, which will also improve your mood and help reduce feelings of depression, relieve anxiety, and also increase blood and oxygen flow to the brain. Strength training is best done in a circuit approach, of moderate to high intensity level, since this will require you to switch gears throughout the workout, making it more challenging on a mental level. To gain optimal benefits from strength training, you'll want to do it 2–3 times a week.

Yoga or Pilates can be added to your well-rounded fitness program or be the foundation of your routine, adding other modalities to round out your program. If you are experiencing a lot of stress in your life, you may want to add more of this form of exercise. There are a great variety of yoga styles and classes, some very vigorous, some very gentle, and some in between. Be sure to select a class level and style that works for you.

If possible, consider performing your exercises first thing in the morning as often as you can. This will increase the total level of brain activity that's taking place, get your mind focused for the day ahead, and it can also assist with the retention of any new information learned that day.

For the best brain health boosting effects, you'll want to balance exercise with sufficient rest, so that you are coming back to each session ready to give it your all. If you find yourself getting tired, moody, or depressed, you may be doing too much exercise. If this is the case, simply back off your activity levels for a few days and give yourself some rest before resuming a program with less intensity.

Finally, keep in mind that you can begin to see the wonderful brain-boosting benefits of exercise after just one or two sessions, at any age!

---

[1] Atalay, et al.. "Exercise plays a preventative role against Alzheimer's disease." *Journal of Alzheimer's Disease.* 20(3) (2010). 777-83.

[2]   Molteni, R. et al. "Voluntary exercise increases axonal regeneration from sensory neurons." *Proceedings of the National Academy of Sciences In The United States Of America.* 1;101(22), (2004). 8473-8.

[3]   Cabral, Howard J., Ciraulo, Domenic A., Jensen, Eric, et al. *The Journal of Alternative and Complementary Medicine.* 13(4). (May 2007). 419-426.

Chapter 6

THIS IS YOUR BRAIN;

THIS IS YOUR BRAIN ON STRESS

S tress has long been shown to affect all parts of the body, from muscles to the digestive system. It is no surprise that stress can damage the brain in the short term, and recent scientific studies have shown that even mild stress can, over time, completely alter brain chemistry. This changing of brain function can possibly lead to Alzheimer's or early onset dementia.[1] It may also be responsible for learning inadequacies, and short term, as well as long-term, memory loss. These conditions typically affect older people, and research has shown that it is not normal stress that causes these conditions, but rather a prolonged response to increased levels of the hormone cortisol circulating in the blood, as a result of the body's physiological response to ongoing stress.

To be able to fully understand why stress can wreak havoc on the brain, it is first necessary to understand what the body's response to stress is. When your body receives a threat stimulus, the nervous system and the endocrine system participate in an intricate process of neural inputs and release of hormones. The region of the brain known as the hypothalamus receives the sensory input of the stressor and will then release hormones to activate another area of the brain called the pituitary gland. While this hormone response is taking place, the hypothalamus is also sending a series of nerve signals to the adrenal gland. These nerve impulses trigger the production of epinephrine, or what is commonly referred to as adrenaline. Meanwhile, the activated pituitary gland releases a cell signaler known as ACTH, which travels through the bloodstream to the adrenal glands. At the site of the adrenal cortex, ACTH will bind to receptors and activate the adrenal glands to produce cortisol. Cortisol and epinephrine each have specific effects on the body.

When epinephrine levels increase, energy levels temporarily get a boost. This happens because epinephrine in the liver triggers the breakdown of sugars into glucose. Epinephrine also has a role in the lungs by binding to smooth muscle bronchioles. This causes the muscles to relax and dilates the bronchioles, increasing oxygen in the bloodstream. Epinephrine also binds to pacemaker cells in the heart, causing the body's heart rate to increase. The increased heart rate allows for larger amounts of oxygen to circulate, resulting in increased muscle energy.

Cortisol also works in a similar fashion. Higher levels of cortisol lead to an increase in gluconeogenesis, which increases blood sugar in the body. It also increases the breakdown and use of proteins, fats, and carbohydrates while suppressing the immune system. These processes allow the body to either fight or flee a stressful or dangerous situation by diverting body resources to energy production and muscle use. This is perfect in the short term to allow the body to rid itself of its stressor. However, long-term stress and long-term activation of these biological pathways may actually be very harmful to your brain. Long-term stress has been the focus of recent scientific research to study and clarify the risks of long-term stress on the body and find out what causes these negative effects.

A recent study conducted by doctors at the University of California, Berkeley has shed some light on why and how prolonged levels of elevated stress can alter brain function[2]. The research showed that chronic stress can lead to an increased production of myelin and a decreased creation of neurons. Myelin is a fatty sheath that surrounds axons giving the networking parts of the brain a white appearance, while an axon is the part of a nerve cell that conducts electrical signals. An overproduction of myelin can throw off the balance between white and gray matter, which, in turn, can affect communication of certain parts of the brain. The difference in the ratio of white and gray matter in the brain caused by these changes can have lasting effects.

Gray matter is the brain structure responsible for storing and processing information, while white matter is made of axons and is responsible for connecting areas of the brain through a network of fibers. White matter gets its name from the white color of myelin. The researchers have thus proposed a mechanism for how this can cause mental disorders such as PTSD and anxiety. If, for example, the connectivity between the hippocampus and the amygdala of the brain are strengthened, this can alter how a brain functions. The hippocampus of the brain is responsible for regulating and managing memories and emotions, while parts of the amygdala are responsible for sensing a fight or flight situation. At the same time, the connection between the hippocampus and prefrontal cortex may be disrupted. The prefrontal cortex is responsible for moderating and inhibiting our emotional responses. In this situation, a person may become exposed to a stressor with its ability to inhibit the stress response diminished, and the amygdala's ability to elicit a response increased, causing a person to potentially overreact to a stressor or feel prolonged levels of stress, resulting in the effects of PTSD or anxiety.

This groundbreaking research focused on the stem cells of the hippocampus in adult rats. These cells were believed to solely be the precursor to neurons and astrocytes and, thus, gray matter. Astrocytes are a type of neuronal cell responsible for providing nutrients to the gray matter parts of the brain. However, the researchers found that, under the effects of constant stress, these cells can also mature into oligodendrocytes, which are responsible for the production of the myelin sheath and, thus, the increase in the brain's white matter. It was shown that the increase in the level of cortisol caused by chronic stress caused these stem cells to produce fewer neurons and more myelin causing permanent changes to the make-up of the brain and led to mental problems, such as depression and anxiety. Thus, researchers have shown that prolonged levels of cortisol production in the body caused by the brain's response to stress can permanently alter brain chemistry and function.

Another study, conducted by researchers at the University of Iowa, looked to show the relation of stress and memory loss in older adults3. The study showed that increased levels of cortisol could have a deleterious effect on the synapses in the prefrontal cortex of the brain. Synapses are connectors between cells in the brain that help collect and store information, while the prefrontal cortex is responsible for storing short-term memory information. If the prefrontal cortex synapses are damaged or destroyed by rising cortisol levels in the body, then short-term memory loss would be a common side effect. Researchers believe that after years and years of increased cortisol exposure, synapses in the prefrontal cortex could begin to shrink.

Researchers have also concluded that treatment that lowers the amount of cortisol in the brain of older adults may help with short-term memory loss. They hypothesized that short-term memory loss related to cortisol activity in the brain starts at age 65 in a human subject. They also hypothesized that the onset of memory loss would appear much more dramatically in those that had a prolonged period of stress in their lives and, thus, increased cortisol levels. The researchers took 21-month-old rats as a comparison. They tested these rats against groups of 4-month-old rats, which would represent a 21-year-old human subject. The rats were further separated into groups depending on their natural level of corticosterone, which is the rat equivalent of cortisol. These groups were then placed in a maze that relied on their short-term memory to complete and receive a treat. The rats were subjected to this maze test at 30, 60 and 120-second intervals. As time went on between maze runs, each group of rats had a general decrease in performance. However, the rats that were older and had the highest levels of corti-

*Another study that showed people who lived **stressful lives**, that is if they experienced family death, hardship, and depression, **were three times more likely to develop Alzheimer's.***

costerone performed the worst out of all the groups. They could complete the maze around 58 percent of the time, while the older rats with low levels of corticosterone could complete the maze at an 80 percent success rate.

After the experiments were completed, the rats were dissected, and their prefrontal cortexes were examined under a microscope. The researchers discovered that the older rats with higher levels of corticosterone had approximately 20 percent fewer synapses in their prefrontal cortexes. This showed a link in corticosterone and memory loss. However, what was also interesting is that older rats that did not have elevated levels of corticosterone showed no signs of memory loss and had their synapses intact. The levels of corticosterone in younger rats did not affect their memory as they all ran the maze with comparable completion percentages. This shows that cortisol's effect on short-term memory loss may be exacerbated by the age of the subject. In any case, a link between the body's response to stress and increased cortisol production has now been linked to another negative effect on the brain's prefrontal cortex, which, in turn, dampens short-term memory.

Unfortunately, increased levels of cortisol caused by stress do not just create the problem of short-term memory loss, but cortisol can also play a role in dementia and Alzheimer's disease.[4] Research conducted at U.C. Irvine has shown a strong link between cortisol and Alzheimer's disease. It has long been shown that patients who are battling Alzheimer's have an increased level of cortisol in their blood stream. However, the mechanism by which cortisol played a role in Alzheimer's formation had yet to be understood.

Alzheimer's is caused by sticky proteins or plaques that are produced in the brain. These plaques disrupt neural connections and cause the memory loss you see in those diagnosed with Alzheimer's. There are two types of proteins that are largely responsible for this disruption. The first is called amyloid beta peptide or Ab. The second is referred to as "tau." Ab will stick in between neurons and while there will cause intercellular plaques and disruptions. Tau actually works inside of a neuron and disrupts a neuron's typical function. These two proteins work in tandem to cause memory loss, irritability, and mood swings often seen in Alzheimer's sufferers.

U.C. researchers showed that individual cells, when exposed to increased levels of cortisol, produced more Ab plaques. The next step for the researchers was to test their findings on animals and, in this case, use a genetically modified mouse.

This mouse was created to show signs and symptoms of Alzheimer's disease as it got older. Young mice were given cortisol every day for a weeks' time before they were old enough to actually show signs of Alzheimer's disease. A week after injection, the mice were euthanized and dissected. The mice given the injections of cortisol showed that in as little as one week from the time of injections, there was a rapidly elevated production of tau and Ab proteins present. If increased amounts of circulating cortisol in the human body cause the increase in the Alzheimer's-causing plaques, it would logically show that an increase in cortisol levels could cause an increased risk of Alzheimer's disease. These results were very consistent with another study that showed people who lived stressful lives, that is if they experienced family death, hardship, and depression, were three times more likely to develop Alzheimer's. Again, a prolonged body response to stress has been linked to poor brain health in humans, especially those who have aged.

While the culprit in negative effects on brain chemistry due to stress has been predominately cortisol, researchers at U.C. Irvine have also pinpointed a hormone responsible for impairment of short-term memory during an acute stress response for subjects at any age.[5]

Researchers discovered that hormones referred to as corticotropin-releasing hormones, or CRHs, can disrupt the body's ability to store memories. It has been previously explained that learning and memory take place at neuronal synapses. Synapses are located on specialized neuronal cells called dendrites. In studies conducted on rats and mice, researchers showed that during stressful events, the body releases CRHs in the hippocampus. During these stressful events, it was shown that the binding of CRHs in neurons causes the degradation of dendrites and thus causes disruption of synapses. This disruption was shown to cause short-term memory loss in the mice and rats. By limiting CRHs in the mice and rats, researchers were able to restore the dendrites, reversing the synaptic damage, and restoring short-term memory function. Limiting the effect of CRHs in dendrites is now a target of further research. Researchers now believe that by reducing the number of CRH receptors available in a person experiencing prolonged levels of high stress, they may be able to reduce short-term memory loss and improve cognitive functioning.

Keep in mind that a body's response to stress is not typically a bad thing. In fact, an increased energy level with increased muscular

Chronic stress can also have an effect on autoimmune diseases.

functioning can be lifesaving in times of physical or emotional hardship. Allowing your body to be more alert and aware with the fight or flight response has been an evolutionary mechanism that has helped the human species to thrive under some of the harshest conditions on the planet. However, prolonged stress can cause immune system dysfunction, high blood pressure, and, as illustrated, completely alter your brain chemistry. Research in mice and humans has found links and shown the mechanisms of action of prolonged stress on numerous mental disorders and conditions. Memory loss, anxiety, depression, and Alzheimer's disease have all been linked to high cortisol levels in the blood, which is a direct result of the body's prolonged response to stress.

Research has also shown that the negative effects of stress are much more prevalent in older people as normal stress doesn't create the same problems as a lifetime of stress does. Much like a dam that has a small crack in it, which builds to a large hole over time, constant stress on your body can eventually wear down the cells and neuronal connections in your brain to the point where a disorder is imminent. Luckily, researchers have begun to understand your brain's response to stress, and cortisol levels seem to be the main antagonist. Further research is being done to see if cortisol-reducing treatments can be effective in reducing symptoms in a person who has shown diminishing cognitive function. Early results are promising.

How to deal with stress

If you are experiencing a lot of stress in your life you are in very good company. In fact, studies show that as many as 117 million adults in the U.S. have reported high levels of anxiety and it is estimated that as much as 70% of the visits to doctors' offices are because of stress related problems. In an effort to feel less stressed several billion dollars were spent by Americans on prescription tranquilizers and antidepressants last year. These enormous expenditures don't include over the counter remedies or other attempts to self-medicate with the use of alcohol or recreational drugs. The good news is that there is a lot you can do about stress and start feeling good again, but before we discuss that, it is helpful to understand how you experience stress and where your stress many be coming from.

What are the symptoms of stress?

Most of us are familiar with common symptoms of stress and have experienced them at one time or another: tight shoulders, tight neck, tight back, headache, stomach problems, irritability, anxiousness, lack of energy, inability to focus or concentrate, and a general lack of satisfaction with life. When stress is chronic (ongoing) it can result in insomnia, high blood pressure, gastrointestinal problems including stomach ulcers and irritable bowel syndrome, weight gain or weight loss, heart disease, stroke, anxiety disorders, depression, burn-out, adrenal exhaustion, sexual dysfunction, inability to get pregnant, decreased ability of the immune system to fight off infections, increased sensitivity to pain, and skin problems.

Chronic stress can also have an effect on auto-immune diseases such as Lupus or rheumatoid arthritis – increasing the likelihood of flare-ups and symptoms. As indicated early in this chapter stress actually accelerates the aging process.

How does stress show up in your life?

- Tense muscles: tight shoulders, tight neck, tight back, etc.
- Headaches
- Lack of appetite
- Stomach problems
- Irritability.
- Anxiety
- Feeling sad or depressed
- Difficulty sleeping
- Easily overwhelmed.
- Lack of energy
- Inability to focus or concentrate
- Lack of satisfaction with life
- High blood pressure
- Feeling burnt out
- Lack of interest in pleasurable activities or hobbies
- Skin problems
- Weight gain or weight loss

What other ways do you experience stress?

Where does stress come from?

Work

- Long hours
- Unsupportive management
- Lack of upward mobility
- Lack of resources/training
- Personality not matched to job
- Job task not clearly defined
- Job loss
- Poor ergonomics /repetitive stress injuries
- Company restructuring such as mergers or downsizing

Environment

- Crowded living areas
- Traffic
- Noise
- Pollution

Stress hardiness is influenced by

- Genetic predisposition to handle stress
- Ability to solve problems and access resources
- Extent of unresolved or unconscious issues from childhood

- Health related issues
- Being overweight
- Substance abuse
- Smoking
- Serious medical issues

Lifestyle

- Major life transitions: marriage, moving, changing jobs, birth of a child, divorce,
- death of a loved one, retirement, etc.
- No time to relax and enjoy life
- Little time for hobbies
- No vacations or breaks from work

Nutrition and exercise

- Poor diet – skipping meals and junk food
- No regular exercise

Quality of relationships with friends, loved ones and family

- Relational conflict
- Lack of social support
- Isolation

Our capacity to successfully deal with stress is called "stress hardiness."

Financial and legal stressors

- Law suits
- Major financial decisions/ obligations
- Having enough money to meet day-to-day living expenses

Other sources of stress

- Natural disasters such as earthquakes, fires, and floods
- Life threatening experiences e.g. car accidents, shootings, war
- Sexual, physical, or emotional abuse, and neglect including abandonment
- Witnessing violence
- Domestic violence
- Rape
- Harassment and intimidation

What stressors do you have in your life?

Your plan for dealing with stress

Step 1. Identifying your stressors. Sometimes stress has become such a regular part of our lives that we accept it as part of living. Therefore, it is vitally important that you take a few moments with the previous sections to identify where your stress is coming from and what impact it has on your life. Doing this can be an eye opening experience and provide you the exact intervention you need to reduce stress and feel better. For example, if you identified that you are not sleeping well (which by itself can cause stress) and you trace this to a noisy air conditioning compressor, then the cure is simple – getting the air conditioner repaired. Granted it is not always this easy, and often there are multiple stressors, but whatever your situation is, it is essential to identify where your stress is coming from and then you will have some idea as to what to do next. It may be an easy fix or it may be something that requires long term planning which will be addressed shortly.

Step 2. Building stress hardiness and minimizing the affects of stress. Stress is an inevitable part of living and we all experience it at various levels of intensity throughout our lives. Our capacity to successfully deal with stress is called "stress hardiness." While each of us has an inherent level of stress hardiness, we can build upon this which helps to minimize the affects of stress, bring balance back into your mind and body, and increase your capacity to handle stressors. Below is a list of very effective ways to build stress hardiness. Select one or two every day and notice how it helps to lower your overall stress levels.

a) Exercise (could be a simple as going for a short walk).

b) Mind-body modalities such as yoga, Pilates, Tai Chi, etc.

c) Meditation.

d)   Soaking in a warm bath.

e) Find a stress management buddy. When you feel overwhelmed have someone

f) listen to you for 5 minutes without interruption. Their job is just to listen, not

g) offer advice.

h) Get a chair massage or exchange a neck and shoulder massage with someone.

i) Rent a funny video or book on tape.

j) Plan a getaway or short trip – just knowing that you will be going will make you feel better!

k) Engage in a hobby. Is there something you have been wanting to do for a long time but for one reason or another haven't gotten to it? Now is the time!

l) Do something nice for someone else. It will feel good!

m) Smile – even if you are not happy. The muscle changes in your face will send a powerful message to your brain and you will feel better instantly.

n) Essential oils have long been used to affect mood. Try lavender, jasmine, or valerian to relax. Use balsam fir or peppermint to energize and uplift your mood.

o) Explore the incredible world of teas. Slow down and enjoy a cup of chamomile tea for relaxation or green tea for a feel good lift. Tea also offers many heath benefits.

p) Read an inspiring book or listen to your favorite music; both proven stressbusters!

q) Check your diet. Be sure to get plenty of vegetables, fruits, whole grains, quality sources of protein and healthy fats into your diet everyday (see the chapter on nutrition). Avoid eating processed foods, white flour products, sugar and transfats. These items in and of themselves will cause health problems and rob you of energy and the nutrition you need to deal with stress. If you need help in this area, consider meeting with a nutritionist.

Step 3. Long range planning for stress. Stress management often requires a long range approach to deal head on with the actual cause of your stressors. For example, if you are retired, single and living in a 3500 square foot home, the regular maintenance and financial aspects of having the house may cause a lot of stress. So long term solutions are needed. You might consider taking in a roommate, selling the house and downsizing, renting it, or refinancing it. Perhaps you are stuck in a job that you really hate, what plans can you start making now to get out that job. How can you transition? Do you need more education, new skills, an updated resume? How do you need to set up your financial situation so that you can comfortably leave your job? By identifying your stressors and developing a plan, you are well on your way to dealing effectively with stress. Even just the act of creating plan created will help you feel better!

Sometimes it takes a team approach to deal with stressors in our lives, especially when you need a little guidance or additional support. Reaching out to the following resources can be particularly helpful:

- Your doctor or health care practitioner
- Psychologist , social worker, or counselor
- Nutritionist

- Attorney
- Financial planner or accountant
- Family
- Friends

---

[1] Bergland, Christopher. "Chronic Stress Can Damage Brain Structure and Connectivity." *Psychology Today* (February 2014). http://www.psychologytoday.com/blog/the-athletes-way/201402/chronic-stress-can-damage-brain-structure-and-connectivity.

[2] Chattarji, Sumantra, Ghosh, Supriya, and Laxmi, Rao. "Functional Connectivity from the Amygdala to the Hippocampus Grows Stronger after Stress." *Journal of Neuroscience* (April 2013). http://www.jneurosci.org/content/33/17/7234.abstract

[3] Mattson, Amy. "Stress hormone linked to short-term memory loss as we age." *Iowa Now* (June 2014). http://now.uiowa.edu/2014/06/stress-hormone-linked-short-term-memory-loss-we-age.

[4] "Stress and Its Influence on Alzheimer's Disease." *UC Irvine.* http://www.mind.uci.edu/stress-and-its-influence-on-alzheimer%E2%80%99s-disease/

[5] Nauert, Rick. "Stress Affects Learning and Memory." *PsychCentral* (March 2008). http://psychcentral.com/news/2008/03/12/stress-affects-learning-and-memory/2031.html.

Chapter 7

WE ARE SOCIAL ANIMALS

THE IMPORTANCE OF SOCIAL CONNECTIONS

Interacting with others can greatly improve your brain's working memory as well as the speed of mental processing.

Aristotle famously said, "Man is by nature a social animal." He was, of course, referring to the fact that socialization is a key characteristic of what makes us human. Today, modern science has confirmed what Aristotle theorized thousands of years ago, and numerous studies into the relationship between brain health and social connections have produced profound implications. As you will see in this chapter, overwhelming scientific evidence suggests that having quality social connections is a central requirement for maintaining brain health, and this becomes even more important as we grow older. There are three primary ways social connections affect brain health: cognitive functioning, mental health, and memory.

Improving Cognitive Functioning

A University of Michigan study, carried out by Psychologist Oscar Ybarra, concluded that social connections play a significant role in improving a person's general cognitive functioning.[101] The study measured the relationship of social engagement and cognitive functioning. Social engagement was defined by how often participants reported speaking on the phone to neighbors, friends, or family; how often they got together;

and the number of people they identified as "close or intimate" – in the sense that they could share their private thoughts, feelings, or concerns. The "cognitive functioning" was defined by problem solving, working memory, cognition, and creative thinking. 3,617 people between 24 and 96 years of age were involved in the study. Physical variables such as physical health and the level of physical activity were taken into account, as well as demographic factors, such as age, gender, level of education, social status, income, marital status, and ethnicity/race. The participants received a number of cognitive tests including a mental exam and a series of arithmetic tests aimed at finding out their level of cognition, problem solving capacity, and working memory. The participants' test results were then correlated with their levels of social interaction.

Not surprisingly, Ybarra concluded that social interaction can have a significant effect on cognitive functioning, impacting memory, cognition, and problem solving. While reflecting on the study, Ybarra famously said, "Most advice for preserving and enhancing mental function emphasizes intellectual activities, such as reading, doing crossword puzzles, and learning how to use a computer. But my research suggests that just getting together and chatting with friends and family may also be effective."

Another study also performed in 2008 by Oscar Ybarra in conjunction with Piotr Winkielman, a psychologist at the University of California, San Diego, proved that even a 10-minute social interaction can greatly improve aspects of cognitive functioning, such as working memory and mental processing speed.

The study was carried out on a group of 76 participants aged between 18 and 21 years. The participants were divided into three groups. One group was allowed to participate in a social interaction for 10 minutes. During the interaction, they would mix with their friends and discuss social issues of interest. The second group was given a number of intellectual tasks. These tasks included solving crossword puzzles and reading comprehension. They were basically supposed to accomplish three intellectual tasks. The third group (control group) was given a film to watch.

Each of the participants was then subjected to two tests. The first one tested their working memory, and the second one tested the speed of their mental processing. On average, the participants in the third group had the worst perfor-

People 60 and above who lack social support are more likely to experience **depression.**

mances in both tests. Those who had participated in social interaction had scores at par with those who were given the intellectual tasks.

The study's findings demonstrated that social interaction can improve cognitive functioning and interacting with others can greatly improve your brain's working memory as well as the speed of mental processing.

Improving Mental Health

A number of symptoms often accompany mental health issues, such as the inability to focus, forgetfulness, moodiness, sleeplessness, anxiety, depression, etc. These symptoms can and do directly affect cognitive performance –our ability to think clearly, solve problems, utilize memory, and function well in everyday life.

For several decades, both psychologists and psychiatrists have emphasized the importance of social interaction in the prevention and treatment of mental health problems, such as depression, anxiety, and severe stress. A 2014 publication by the National Institute of Mental Health (NIMH) reported that mental disorders can directly affect the brain and thus negatively impact brain functions, such as cognition, memory, perception, and executive function.[102]

According to a 2013 WHO study entitled "Depression and Older Adults," people 60 and above who lack social support are more likely to experience depression as their counterparts who have adequate social support.[103] Indeed, people who are lonely or lacking social support are more prone to chronic stress, anxiety and depression, and those people who have strong social support networks are less likely to experience mental health challenges. However, when older adults are given psychosocial support aimed at encouraging social contact or interaction, they experience less incidences of depression.

Social interaction provides a number of benefits, including an expression and release of your thoughts and feelings and connection to others – realizing you are not alone, that others have similar problems, and you are able to get practical solutions to problems. Engaging in social activities may also help you forget your problems (at least temporarily) and enjoy yourself, thereby increasing positive feelings and connections.

Not surprisingly, social support is at the core of most mental health therapy and usually contains an emphasis on encouraging and empowering patients to form supportive social relationships. Talk therapy is in itself a social interaction. Think about it!

Improving Memory

Social connections also offer the additional benefits of an improved memory and delay the onset of age-induced memory degeneration. This was the conclusion of a study carried out by researchers at the Harvard School of Public Health.[104] The purpose of the study was to find out if social integration had any impact on age-induced memory loss.

The researchers measured social integration based on marital status; contact with parents, children, siblings or neighbors; and active participation in volunteer activities. Memory was assessed four times over a six-year period with subjects 50 years of age or older. In one of the tests, a list of 10 common nouns was read to each participant. The participant was then asked to recall as many nouns as possible immediately after hearing the list, and again after a period of five minutes. The researchers controlled for variables like gender, ethnicity, income levels, and social status.

The results of the study showed that those with the most social integration had the slowest rate of memory decline. In fact, memory decline among the most socially active was less than half the rate of those who were the least socially integrated. These findings were independent of socio-demographic factors, such as age, gender, and race. The impact is even more pronounced for people who have had little formal education (considered as less than 12 years of schooling).

"Social participation and integration have profound effects on health and well-being of people during their lifetimes," said Lisa F. Berkman, the senior author of the study. "We know from previous studies that people with many social ties have lower mortality rates. We now have mounting evidence that strong social networks can help to prevent declines in memory. As our society ages and has more and more older people, it will be important to promote their engagement in social and community life to maintain their well-being."

It is this active participation in life's affairs that enables a person to benefit from the memory-boosting effects of social interaction. People in their 50s or 60s who are actively engaged in their family, community, and/or social life will benefit more than someone who is isolated or takes a passive role when it comes social interactions. Ultimately, it is not the mere presence of being around other people that matters. It is how active someone is in their social interactions that produces the benefits.

This is perfectly illustrated in a program for Alzheimer's patients developed by Dr. Sharon Arkin, a psychiatrist at the University of Arizona.[105] The program basically involves engaging the patients in communal exercise sessions with a group of college students. The patients get to interact, exercise, and just have a jolly good time with the students. She has documented evidence that these exercise sessions not only improve the patients' moods but also slow down the progress of Alzheimer's disease-related memory loss.

Getting and staying connected

There are different avenues through which you can form such social connections. The best and easiest way is by taking an active interest in family life, if possible. If your spouse or children are around, it is helpful to participate in discussions around key family decisions. Rather than taking the backseat (which many retirees do), it is valuable to get engaged and share your opinions, vision, and wisdom. Given the wealth of experience most older people have, they are in a great position to offer insightful advice.

Another way is by getting involved with social causes. This can include serious things like volunteering for socially-driven organizations or charities or could be more recreational like organizing oldies music get-togethers. Whether it is putting together free meals for the homeless or gathering a group of friends for a game of bridge, the most important thing is taking part in something that involves other people. The end result will not only improve the functioning of your brain, but you'll also be having fun while making the world a better place.

Ultimately, as the poet John Donne eloquently put it, "No man is an island." And establishing social connections is essential to what makes us human. These connections can greatly impact our brain health and our memory, problem solving, speed of mental processing, and general cognitive functioning.

[1]   Mental Exercising Through Simple Socializing: Social Interaction Promotes General Cognitive. Oscar Ybarra, Eugene Burnstein, Piotr Winkielman, Matthew C. Keller, Melvin Manis, Emily Chan and Joel Rodriguez. Pers Soc Psychol Bull 2008; 34; 248

[2]   Hitti FL, Siegelbaum SA. The Hippocampal CA2 Region is Essential for Social Memory. Nature , published online February 23, 2014.http://www.nimh.nih.gov/news/science-news/2014/brain-region-singled-out-for-social-memory-possible-therapeutic-target-for-select-brain-disorders.shtml

[3]   http://www.who.int/mediacentre/factsheets/fs381/en/

[4] Effects of Social Integration on Preserving Memory Function in a Nationally Representative U.S. Elderly Population," Karen A. Ertel, M. Maria Glymour, Lisa F. Berkman, American Journal of Public Health, July 2008, Vol. 98, No. 7. (doi: 10.2105/ AJPH.2007.113654)

[5] http://www.u.arizona.edu/~sarkin/elderrehab.html

Chapter 8

ZZZZZ'S

SLEEP IS VERY GOOD FOR YOUR BRAIN

As we age, the amount of time spent in the **deep stages** *of sleep decreases.*

40 percent of adults in the U.S. get less than the recommended and needed 7–9 hours of sleep, and according to the National Sleep Foundation, 58 percent of adults in the U.S report having symptoms of insomnia a few nights a week or more.[1] Symptoms include not being able to get to sleep, frequently waking up during the night, waking up and not being able to get back to sleep, waking up early, and not being able to getting enough refreshing sleep. Baby boomers are particularly susceptible to getting less than the required amount of quality sleep each night as the need for sleep does not decline with an increase in age.

In fact, not only does insomnia favor those over 50, but often the quality of sleep we get is diminished. Just because you went to sleep at a reasonable hour and woke up at a designated time in the morning, doesn't mean that your brain and body received adequate sleep. You might need to spend more time in bed to get the right amount of sleep.[2]

As we age, the amount of time spent in the deep stages of sleep decreases, changing the length and quality of sleep. Sleep tends to be lighter, more fractionated with an increased number of awakenings, and not as refreshing. Additionally, the causes for insomnia, which are experienced with greater frequency, include medical issues, such as arthritis, osteoporosis, cancer, gastro-intestinal problems; respiratory issues, such as asthma or wheezing; dementia, diabetes, heart disease, menopause, frequent urination, and increased medication use.

Seniors generally experience more aches and pains, which makes getting a good night's sleep more challenging. Psychological issues, such as dealing with grief, depression, isolation, and anxiety are also more common later in life and can have a direct impact on sleep.

There is also a reduction in the production of hormones including melatonin, which is a chemical messenger that is sent throughout your body and mind to prepare you for sleep. As we age, a reduction in brain cells may also occur, which is a contributing factor to poor sleep. Additionally, exercise and activity levels, which are important for a good night's sleep, tend to be generally lower as we grow older.

A research study by the University of Washington School of Medicine in St. Louis suggests that people who awaken more during the night are more likely than sound sleepers to have pre-clinical signs of Alzheimer's disease. Those waking up more than five times in an hour had an increased risk of having a build-up of amyloid plaque in their brains, which is linked to Alzheimer's disease.

People who awaken more during the night are more likely than sound sleepers to have pre-clinical signs of Alzheimer's disease.

Sleep and brain health as we age; sleep deprivation is a serious problem

Nearly 75 percent of all adults in their 50s report getting less than seven hours of sleep, while 25 percent of them believe that they suffer from a sleep disorder. During a normal night, we go through five stages of sleep.[3] Together, these form one sleep cycle, which lasts for 90 minutes, and during one night, people go through 4–5 such sleep cycles.[4]

Stages 1 and 2 are linked to light sleep, while stages 3 and 4 are when people sleep deeply. Together, these four stages are called NREM, or non-rapid eye movement. The fifth stage of sleep is known as REM, or rapid eye movement; this is the dreaming stage in which our brain is the most relaxed.

A decline in the quality of sleep means that the amount of time spent in the deep sleep stages goes down. With age, it is common for most people to spend less time in stages 3 and 4, as people tend to wake more from the issues mentioned above.

In other words, for x amount of time you spend in bed, the amount of deep, restful, and beneficial sleep declines.

How much sleep is needed?

While an average adult needs 7–9 hours of sleep, there are those individuals who can put in peak performance even with six hours of sleep. Then, there are others who need to spend at least nine hours in bed to feel rested. The amount of sleep you need is not a matter of preference; it depends on genetics and hereditary factors. So, the optimal number of sleeping hours will vary from one person to another.

The simplest way to understand how much sleep you need is to listen to what your body is telling you. If you need a jolt of caffeine or the shrill cry of an alarm clock to shock you out of bed, you are obviously not getting as much sleep as your body needs. If you find yourself napping frequently, this is another telltale sign of sleep deprivation, apart from fatigue or medical issues.

Sleep deprivation negatively affects your brain

Not getting enough sleep is a common occurrence for many people, and most of them live under the misconception that they have trained their bodies to not need as much sleep. But this could not be further from the truth; in essence, what you are doing is forcing yourself to stay awake. With reduced sleep or extended periods of wakefulness, neurons begin to malfunction. Unlike the other muscles in the body that can regenerate at rest, the only way you can relax and renew your brain is through sleep.[5]

Even when you are resting, your brain, particularly the cerebral cortex, continues to be in a semi-alert state. So, just resting without physical movement is not something that works for the brain. Only the various stages of deep sleep contribute toward the regeneration of neurons, sorting and forming of new memories, and the development of new synaptic connections. This means that unless you are sleeping enough, these functions are being impacted negatively.

Various research studies have shown that prolonged lack of adequate sleep affects the brain in the following ways:

Not getting enough sleep is a common occurrence for many people.

The center of the brain that is linked to linguistic processing, the temporal lobe, is severely impacted: In subjects who were fully rested and put through a verbal learning/reasoning exam, the MRI (magnetic resonance imaging) scan showed activity in the temporal lobe while people were going through the test.[6] However, in sleep-deprived individuals, this section of the cerebral cortex failed to light up.

The physical impact of sleep deprivation, which often involves slurred speech, can be attributed to the inactivity in this part of the brain. Yet, even people who are severely sleep-deprived were able to perform to some extent on the verbal learning test. Since the temporal lobe is not handling this task in these individuals, it is obvious that some other part of the brain is compensating for it.

The parietal lobe showed activity, which meant that it was handling the workload of the temporal lobe. However, what needs to be understood is that although the parietal lobe compensates for the lack of temporal functioning, it is not primarily designed to handle the task. This would explain why sleep deprived subjects did not perform as well on the test as their rested counterparts. Of course, the fact that there was a reduction in the regeneration of neurons also added to the woes of subjects who did not get enough sleep.

To put it simply, without sleep, the various parts of the brain do not function as they should. While some shut down, others are overworked. Also, the control shift from one area of the brain to the other means a time lag, which is why people with an increased degree of sleep deprivation perform progressively worse, not only on verbal reasoning tests, but also on math and critical thinking exercises.[7]

Sleep deprivation leads to brain damage: A study published in the Journal of Neuroscience revealed that trying to make up sleep debt by oversleeping through the weekend is a futile endeavor. The study showed that sleep was essential for metabolic homeostasis of the neurons. Wakefulness causes mitochondrial stress, which means the neurons start to degenerate. Unfortunately, the damage done cannot be reversed by getting more than the requisite amount of sleep on some days.[8]

To understand the precise impact of wakefulness on the life of the neurons, mice were subjected to irregular sleep schedules, much like shift workers. The rodents actually lost 25 percent

Sleep deprivation leads to brain damage.

of the neurons from the locus coeruleus, the center of the brain linked to wakefulness and certain cognitive functions.

It was found that for the first few days, the production of the protein needed to energize and protect the mice would be stepped up by the new brain cells to compensate for the lack of sleep. But consistent sleep deprivation lowered protein production, and the neurons began to die at a faster pace.[9]

The link between Alzheimer's and sleep deprivation[10]: A report published in the Journal of Neurobiology of Aging suggested that people with chronic sleep deprivation were more likely to develop Alzheimer's and would develop the disease sooner than those who slept well. The study involved two groups of mice: one was exposed to 12 hours of light and 12 hours of darkness, while the other was subjected to 20 hours of light and 4hours of darkness.

The lack of darkness understandably reduced sleep time. At the end of the eight-week period, the rodents who slept less were found to have significant deterioration in memory; their ability to learn new things was also impaired despite both groups having the same amount of amyloid plaque in the brain, which is a hallmark of Alzheimer's.

Increase in irritability[11]: Being around sleep-deprived people is not a pleasant experience as they are often on the edge and irritated. While people assume that a good night's sleep will take care of the foul mood, prolonged sleep deprivation can have a long standing psychological impact, including an increased risk of suicide.

Cognitive impairment: The prefrontal cortex, which handles all of the executive functions for the brain, such as decision-making and problem solving, gets severely impaired due to lack of sleep. This means that without the requisite number of zzzs, your day to day functioning is going to take a hit.

Memory loss: As mentioned earlier, sleep deprivation causes the degeneration of neurons, which, in turn, impacts long-term memory. Even short-term memory is impacted by lack of sleep as fewer synaptic connections are built, leading to poor memory recall.[12]

Hand-eye coordination declines: There is a reason why you shouldn't be driving or operating heavy machinery when sleep deprived. Your response time will be very similar to that of a person who has consumed alcohol. Very dangerous!

Hallucinations: It may start with quick sightings of a flashing or moving light in your vision field, but the longer you go without adequate sleep, the more severe and frequent the hallucinations get.

The immune system is compromised: Lack of sleep not only slows down the activity of existing white blood cells, but it also decreases their production in the body. Additionally, when your brain is sleep-deprived, the secretion of the growth hormone is reduced. This impacts your body's ability to metabolize sugar. In fact, so serious are the results of sleep deprivation on the body that individuals who get less than four hours of sleep per day are 75 percent more likely to die within the next six years.[13]

Increased susceptibility to type 2 diabetes: Shorter sleeping periods lead to higher resistance to insulin, which is the leading cause of type 2 diabetes.

Development of arrhythmias: Decreased sleep also impacts the functioning of the sinus node of the heart, which controls the rhythm of heart beats. So, blood pressure issues and an increased heart rate are common among people who are not getting enough sleep. In fact, not getting enough sleep can raise your risk of developing a cardiac issue by almost 48 percent.

Not getting enough quality rest can result in a host of severe negative consequences to your brain as well as your overall health.

Can cause the onset of osteoporosis: The lack of quality sleep also impacts bone health. This is particularly poignant for women in their 50s as it can compound the skeletal problems caused by menopause and hormonal changes.[14]

Make you look older: While hair graying and some wrinkles are common as you hit the fifth decade of your life, not getting enough sleep can actually make you look older and exacerbate these signs of aging. As an excessive amount of cortisol, which is the stress hormone, gets secreted in response to the lack of sleep, the cells in the body fail to regenerate as usual. This, in turn, can cause premature hair graying and the appearance of wrinkles, and, of course, under-eye dark circles.[15]

Increases risk of obesity: Like many other physiological functions, sleep deprivation also impacts the digestive process, slowing down the metabolism of certain nutrient groups. This will cause you to put on weight. Also, cortisol is known to create cravings, and once you succumb to these, weight gain is imminent.

Now you can see that not getting enough quality rest can result in a host of severe negative consequences to your brain as well as your overall health. It is vital and essential to make a good night's sleep a priority. We need good quality, restful sleep to feel our best and maintain health and to renew and rebalance our brains, bodies, and emotions.

If you have trouble getting a good night's sleep, here are a variety of proven tips to make sure the sandman pays you a visit

Go to sleep and wake up at the same time every day (even on weekends). This will help reset your sleep-wake cycle. The best time for most people to go to sleep is between 10:00–11:00 p.m., and the best time to awaken is between 6:00–7:00 a.m. Avoid napping if you have trouble sleeping.

Exercise. Even a short 20-minute walk will work. This will help reduce your stress hormones, clear your mind, and make you more tired at bedtime. Be careful not to exercise vigorously too close to bedtime, though, as it may have just the opposite effect and make you feel more energized.

Turn off electronics. The light coming from your television is very stimulating to the visual cortex of your brain – the last thing you need late at night. Experiment with turning off your television by 9:00 p.m. This goes for surfing the Internet, too! Try it for a week or two and see what happens.

Turn down the lights. Your body and mind take signals from the environment. Melatonin is a hormone that informs your system that it is time to sleep and is triggered by darkness. Being in a well-lighted environment throughout the night is counter-productive to relaxing and falling asleep. Try lighting some candles.

Listen to soft music. Researchers in Japan have found that listening to soft, relaxing music is a highly effective way to fall asleep.

Herbs and tea. Chamomile tea is a time-proven remedy for relaxing. Other herbs that work well include hops, passionflower, and valerian. These herbs are also readily available as capsules or tinctures.

Ditch the caffeine. Caffeine can remain in your system for up to 35 hours. That means that cup of coffee you had this morning can keep you awake tonight. Wean yourself off of caffeine with decaf or try herbal teas. Watch out for caffeine in soda, too!

Alcohol. Many people have a drink or two to fall asleep. While it's true the alcohol will help you fall asleep, you'll most likely awaken as it interferes with deeper stages of sleep and can be dehydrating.

Noisy environment. Is there noise coming from inside or outside of your home? We need a quiet environment to sleep well. If there is noise around your bedroom, consider making some adjust-ments: earplugs, a white noise generator, moving your bedroom, etc.

Overactive mind. If your mind won't shut off, get out a pen and paper and write down every-thing going through your mind until it is cleared. Remind yourself that you can deal with these things tomorrow.

Make relaxation, not sleep, your goal. Many people beat themselves up if they can't fall asleep, only making the situation worse. Remember that nobody has died as a result of not sleeping, and that relaxation is the key to falling asleep. If you can relax, sleep will follow naturally. Make relax-ation your goal!

If you suffer from insomnia, would like to know more about what might be keeping you from sleep, and want to discover additional ways to get to a good night's sleep, please take a look at my book: *Insomnia: How Can I Get to Sleep? Your Guide to Overcoming Insomnia, Sleeplessness, and Getting a Good Night Sleep.* Available on Amazon.

---

[1] Jones, Jeffrey M. "In U.S., 40% Get Less Than Recommended Amount of Sleep." *Gallup Wellness* (2013). http://www.gallup.com/poll/166553/less-recommended-amount-sleep.aspx

2   Gibbons, Michael. "Baby Boomers Hit Prime Age for Sleep Disorders." *Advance for Managers of Respiratory Care* (June 2006). http://www.health.txstate.edu/rc/contentParagraph/06/document/Sleep%20&%20Baby%20Boomers.PDF.

3   Nguyen, Linda. "Inability to sleep increases suicide risk for baby boomers." *Tech Times* (August 2014). http://www.techtimes.com/articles/12984/20140814/inability-to-sleep-increases-suicide-risk-for-baby-boomers.htm

4   Shaw, Gina. "Sleep Through the Decades." *WebMD*. http://www.webmd.com/sleep-disorders/features/adult-sleep-needs-and-habits

5   Klemm, William. "Is Lack of Sleep Causing Your Brain to Shrivel?" *Psychology Today* (February 2013). http://www.psychologytoday.com/blog/memory-medic/201302/is-lack-sleep-causing-your-brain-shrivel

6   Harrison, Yvonne and Horne, James A. "Sleep Loss and Temporal Memory." *The Quarterly Journal of Experimental Psychology* (2000). http://www.christofflab.ca/pdfs/2009/01/harrison-horne-2000.pdf

7   Brown, Gregory J., et al. "Altered brain response to verbal learning following sleep deprivation." *Nature* (1999). http://www.nature.com/nature/journal/v403/n6770/full/403655a0.html

8   DeNoon, Daniel J. "Lack of Sleep Takes Toll on Brain Power" *WebMD Health News* (2000). http://www.webmd.com/sleep-disorders/news/20000209/lack-of-sleep-takes-toll-on-brain-power

9   Haiken, Melanie. "Lack Of Sleep Kills Brain Cells, New Study Shows." *Forbes* (March 2014) http://www.forbes.com/sites/melaniehaiken/2014/03/20/lack-of-sleep-kills-brain-cells-new-study-suggests/

10   "Sleep Loss May Cause Brain Damage and Accelerate Onset of Alzheimer's, Two New Studies Show." *Mercola* (April 2014).http://articles.mercola.com/sites/articles/archive/2014/04/03/sleep-loss-alzheimers-disease.aspx

11   Breus, Michael J. "Sleep Habits: More Important Than You Think" *WebMD*. http://www.webmd.com/sleep-disorders/features/important-sleep-habits

12   Klein, Sarah. "8 Scary Side Effects Of Sleep Deprivation." *Huffington Post* (April 2013). http://www.huffingtonpost.com/2014/09/18/scary-sleep-deprivation-effects_n_2807026.html

13   Matta, Christy. "8 Effects of Sleep Deprivation on Your Health." *PsychCentral* (March 2013). http://psychcentral.com/blog/archives/2013/02/13/8-effects-of-sleep-deprivation-on-your-health/

14   Altevogt, B.M. and Colten, H.R. "Extent and Health Consequences of Chronic Sleep Loss and Sleep Disorders." *Sleep Disorders and Sleep Deprivation: An Unmet Public Health Problem.* Washington, DC: (2006). http://www.ncbi.nlm.nih.gov/books/NBK19961/

15   "Why lack of sleep is bad for your health." *NHS.* http://www.nhs.uk/livewell/tiredness-and-fatigue/pages/lack-of-sleep-health-risks.aspx

Chapter 9

OM

YOGA AS AN ANTIDOTE
TO AGING

Yoga arrived in the world some 5,000 to 10, 000 years ago. Its purpose and promise was to end suffering and help people extend their lives, so they could burn karma in this lifetime and not have to deal with it in the next. In the process, the ancient yogis developed a host of tools for improving and maintaining the health of the body, mind, and spirit.

Before I say more about yoga, I need to offer this disclosure: I have been practicing yoga for 23 years and teaching it for 18. I have seen the incredible impact it has made in my own life and the lives of my students. I have read tons of yoga books, yoga research, and have attended countless yoga classes, workshops, and trainings. Needless to say, I am very enthusiastic about the benefits of yoga as an antiaging modality. Now, back to this chapter.

What is particularly interesting is that if you overlay the practice of yoga onto the chapters of this book onto you, you can begin to see the power of yoga as an antiaging modality. Let's take a look:

Chapter two: how our brains age. In this chapter, various structures of the brain were discussed as well as how aging affects them. In particular, the shortening of telomere length, and how this triggers more prevalent cell death as we age, was detailed. Having a direct effect on telomeres is an enzyme called telomerase, which helps to rebuild and lengthen telomeres. Interestingly, there is a direct correlation between telomerase activity and psychological well-being, physical health, and longevity. And, in a study performed at U.C. Davis, researchers discovered that meditation directly effects a person's psychological well-being, which in turn affects "telomerase" in immune cells.

It is worth noting that the practice of meditation offers a host of antiaging benefits, including a reduction in stress, lower blood pressure, increased sense of well-being/better moods, enhanced immune system, and reduced risk of age-related dementia. Research is also showing that meditation increases activity of 'natural-killer cells,' which kill bacteria and cancer cells. If you would like to know more about the benefits of meditation and/or how to practice, please take a look at my book: *Meditation, The Gift Inside.* Available on Amazon.

Chapter three: diet. As you may recall, there are certain foods that, over time, diminish your brain's capacity to function well and contribute to aging. These include trans fats, refined flour products, and sugar – essentially, the ingredients in most packaged foods. The yogic diet recommends whole foods: fruits, vegetables, legumes, whole grains, quality dairy products, etc. This is a diet that is consistent with good health, sound nutrition, and the optimum functioning of the brain.

Chapter four: exercise. In this chapter, the role of exercise and activity in brain health was discussed. A regular practice of yoga postures (asanas) has proven to enhance strength, flexibility, and circulation. An asana practice can be vigorous, aerobic, gentle, quieting, energizing, or anything in between. An asana practice can be tailored to just about anyone at any age. Interestingly, there are a group of postures that increase blood flow to the head – these include standing forward bends and inverted postures, such as headstands, shoulder-stands, and handstands.

Yoga postures can be used to prevent, cure, and reduce the symptoms of common physical and emotional issues associated with aging, such as back problems, arthritis, digestive issues, high blood pressure, asthma/breathing problems, depression, moodiness, etc. Asana practice is also very helpful for maintaining a healthy weight.

Yoga postures can be used to prevent, cure, and reduce the symptoms of common physical and emotional issues associated with aging.

Chapter six: stress. When it comes to stress, yoga offers a host of powerful and proven stress-busters, including breathing practices, asana practice (mentioned above), meditation, and chanting. And yoga philosophy can provide you with valuable guidelines for living your life in balance.

Chapter seven: social connections. One of the beautiful things about yoga is that it affects you on all levels – body, mind, emotions, spirit, etc. When you practice yoga, your heart opens to others around you, and it is easier to connect to other human beings. When you come together with other yogis to practice yoga, you take part in a shared activity with common interests and values. It is natural for friendships to grow out of this.

Chapter eight: sleep. The number one reason most people have insomnia or trouble sleeping is due to stress. Once again, yoga offers a wide variety of tools and techniques to help people de-stress, relax deeply, and prepare for sleep. And as mentioned above, yoga can also help with other medical issues which may be causing sleeplessness.

More benefits of yoga: In addition to all of the above, yoga can be used to improve mental focus and concentration and enhance neuromuscular connections. And yoga also provides a fertile ground for learning – there is always something new to learn and discover when you practice and study yoga. I am big fan of the 'use it or lose it' theory.

If you look at people in their later years who have been practicing yoga for a long time versus those who have not, you will notice a huge difference in the way they move and the way they look, their health, and their attitude towards life. If you already practice yoga, keep up the great work; if you have never practiced before, consider giving it a try – you might just find your fountain of youth!

Notes

ADDITIONAL PUBLICATIONS OF INTEREST

Yoga: The Back Pain Cure

Back pain! As anyone with a backache will tell you, pain, limited activities, and days missed from work take their toll physically, financially, and emotionally.

A big problem with most back care programs is limited treatment options. Pain medications often mask problems, allowing further damage to occur because warning pain is not felt. Physical therapy is limited by what insurance companies deem necessary, and lastly, surgery, a costly option, is often ineffective.

The good news is that yoga therapy can help relieve your pain while at the same time improve flexibility and strength. This book features two yoga therapy practices. The first is for acute back problems, which means you're in pain right now. This practice is designed to bring structural balance back into your body and gently stretch key muscles, reducing pain and helping you heal. The second practice is designed to build strength and flexibility, which helps prevent future problems.

Release Your Shoulders, Relax Your Neck: The Best Exercises for Relieving Shoulder Tension and Neck Pain.

Do you suffer from shoulder pain or shoulder tension? How about neck pain?

In this book, discover:

- The main causes of shoulder and neck pain.
- How to eliminate shoulder tension and neck pain with 53 highly effective shoulder and neck exercises.
- Photos of the exercises with easy to follow instructions.
- Key prevention strategies to stop problems before they start.
- Why computer users are at risk for injury and what to do to significantly reduce your risk.
- Anatomy of the shoulder joints, how they move, and why they can get so tight.

This book is a must for dental hygienists, hair stylists, athletes, people who work on computers, and people who carry a lot of stress in their neck or shoulders.

Insomnia: How Can I Get to Sleep?

Lying awake, tossing and turning, mental agitation, and the exhaustion that follows are definitely not a lot of fun!

The side effects of insomnia can reduce your productivity, make you irritable, and lead to numerous physical ailments, including obesity, hypertension, lack of coordination, weight gain, etc.

In this book, you'll discover:

- What is really keeping you up at night; the answer might surprise you!
- The best non-drug methods for getting to sleep naturally with our "Insomnia Tool Box."
- How to get back to sleep when you wake up in the middle of the night.
- How to reduce and eliminate tension and anxiety with powerful techniques that help quiet your mind, remove stress from your body, and slip easily into a good night's sleep.
- How to eat your way to a good night's sleep: which foods actually help you fall asleep and which will keep you from falling asleep.

Meditation: The Gift Inside

For thousands of years, people of faith, ascetics, as well as everyday people, have practiced meditation to quiet their minds, find inner peace, and connect with their spirit.

Whether you are looking for a book on meditation for beginners, or you are an experienced meditator wanting to renew your practice, you'll find "Meditation: The Gift Inside" connects you to the heart of the practice. Discover:

- How to meditate like a yogi: experience the same meditation techniques that the deepest meditators use.
- Uncover the secrets to quiet your mind; have inner peace even when your outer world may be chaotic.
- Powerful methods to deepen meditation.
- How to easily make meditation a part of your daily life and eliminate challenges that may prevent you from practicing.
- The extraordinary benefits of meditation, including sleeping better, reducing pain, improving mood, extending life, etc.

ABOUT THE AUTHOR

Howard VanEs, M.A., E-RYT 500, has been committed to wellness and fitness for over 30 years. He has a deep passion for helping people learn about the many ways they can improve the quality of their health and empower their lives through natural methods of healing.

Howard has written over 19 books, most focused on health and wellness. Many of his books have been best sellers in their respective categories on Amazon. For over 24 years, Howard has been a dedicated practitioner of hatha yoga and has been teaching yoga for the last 19 years in the Bay Area of California. Howard also has a M.A. in counseling psychology and is a former psychotherapist.

Learn more about Howard and his books at www.BooksonHealth.net.